'*Character Toolkit* is an immensely r
of inspiration and guidance for an,
children and young people cultivate vital character virtues that enable
them to flourish.'

– Dr Tom Harrison, Director of Education, Jubilee Centre for
Character and Virtues, University of Birmingham

'The only way the science of character can have a tangible impact in the
classroom is through finding concrete and creative ways to translate it
into practice. This toolkit does just that.'

– Dr Ilona Boniwell, programme leader, MSc in Applied Positive
Psychology, Anglia Ruskin University & CEO of Positran

'A sensationally effective practical toolkit! Roberts and Wright seamlessly
use evidence-based research to introduce a theme and set the context for
the activities, which are clear and quick to read! This really is the text of
my teacher dreams; a multi-layered character education gem that needs
to be on every school bookshelf!'

– Kate Sowter, deputy head, Pathfinder Teaching School,
CPD Lead Pathfinder Multi Academy Trust

'This book is an excellent resource for busy teachers seeking an
introduction to Character and Positive Education. It includes a wealth
of ideas to promote mental health and wellbeing in children, and its
practical activities can be lifted straight off the pages and delivered in
schools and classrooms.'

– Jane Kirkham, psychologist and teacher,
Association of Independent Schools of Western Australia

'The *Toolkit's* many exercises provide school professionals and their pupils
with the necessary guidance to teach and learn differently. Through its
thoroughly researched background information, precise instructions and
– most importantly – sincere empathy, this book strikes me as a perfect
instrument to take simple steps towards great goals.'

– Claire Russon, psychologist, senior research and development advisor,
Ministry of Education, Children and Youth, Luxembourg

'This practical and easily accessible resource is a gift for teachers keen to
grow children's emotional wellbeing. The underlying theory and research
is provided in digestible language, and the practical and fun exercises can
be integrated into the curriculum without burdening our busy teachers.'

– Peter Harper, consultant clinical psychologist and Val Payne,
education consultant; both in independent practice

'The authors have carefully created a brilliant guide. The book expertly provides theories and fun-yet-thought-provoking practical activities in easy, accessible chunks for schools that strive to help each child reach their full potential.'

– Louisa Simons, Lower Key Stage Two Phase Leader and Whole School Growth Mindset Leader, Brodetsky Primary School

'*Character Toolkit* brilliantly combines current research with clear, straightforward classroom activities. This is a practical and invaluable resource for teachers seeking to support students in navigating the school years and beyond.'

– Lauren Knussen, senior research associate & PhD candidate, School of Education, University of Technology Sydney

'Positively practical...perfectly poised to become a primary resource for teachers, practitioners and parents concerned about the social–emotional wellbeing of our children and youth. The activities and resources are easily adaptable to various settings and ages, even my college-level students! '

– Beverley Myatt, MEd, psychology professor, Durham College, Ontario, Canada

'Steeped in research, this toolkit should be essential reading for every school team and integral in the design of a character education curriculum – the foundation on which to help build a school's ethos and culture prioritising wellbeing for children and staff. Roberts and Wright have written a must-read for teachers everywhere.'

– Flora Barton, headteacher, Crowmarsh Gifford C. E. Primary School

'*Character Toolkit* is an essential resource for teachers and school leaders who wish to introduce character and positive education into their classrooms and school environments. Roberts and Wright have provided educators with a broad range of useful, practical and evidence-based activities to assist with the provision of a holistic education which prioritises student and community wellbeing.'

– Rhiannon McGee, Head of Positive Education at Geelong Grammar School

'Frederika and Elizabeth bring to life the theory of character education as bitesize practical chunks in this teacher-friendly guide. I especially like the focus on developing 'emotional granularity' in our learners. If our students can identify, articulate and harness their emotions, they will be able to flourish with mental and physical wealth. '

– Hannah Wilson, executive headteacher, Aureus School & Aureus Primary School

'Every so often you read a book powerful enough to define your pedagogy; *Character Toolkit* is it! It translates an extraordinary amount of outstanding research into simple learning activities that will transform classrooms into places of discovery, joy and fun, and allow students to flourish, grow and positively contribute to society.'

– Vanessa Gamack, mission and education advisor,
Anglican Schools Commission, Southern Queensland

'Character is how we put strengths and values into everyday practice. The earlier children learn these skills, the happier and more meaningful their lives are likely to be. Roberts and Wright have created an excellent resource providing detailed activities to develop a diverse range of character traits.'

– Dr Sue Roffey, FRSA, FBPsS, honorary professor at
Exeter University, Director, Growing Great Schools Worldwide

'This highly accessible book provides a rich set of resources to help students develop a love of learning, a deep sense of connection and an understanding of moral and ethical issues through practices of self-reflection, gratitude and kindness.'

– Professor Penny Jane Burke, Global Innovation Chair of Equity,
Director, Centre of Excellence for Equity in Higher Education (CEEHE)

'*Character Toolkit* is a gift for teachers and anyone who works with children. Roberts and Wright have written an essential guide for teaching character!'

– Caren Baruch-Feldman, PhD, psychologist and author of
The Grit Guide for Teens: A Workbook to Help You
Build Perseverance, Self-Control, and a Growth Mindset

'Found it at last! A toolkit to inspire the next stage of our work on the character education curriculum. As a multi-academy trust with a clear focus on the 'Inner Curriculum' we have been looking for ways to inspire our teams to embed activities to develop specific character traits and positive qualities in our young people. This amazing book is the answer!'

– Stephen Chamberlain, chief executive, Challenger Multi Academy Trust/
Senior Partner: Challenge Partners/National Leader of Governance

'This book provides great ideas and strategies as a vehicle to bring a school's vision to life with impactful character and positive education.'

– Patrick Ottley-O'Connor, executive principal &
leadership development coach

Can I tell you about Compassion?
Sue Webb
ISBN 978 1 78592 466 8
eISBN 978 1 78450 848 7

Can I tell you about Gratitude?
Liz Gulliford
ISBN 978 1 78592 457 6
eISBN 978 1 78450 833 3

How to Be a Peaceful School
Practical Ideas, Stories and Inspiration
Edited by Anna Lubelska
ISBN 978 1 78592 156 8
eISBN 978 1 78450 424 3

The School of Wellbeing
12 Extraordinary Projects Promoting Children and
Young People's Mental Health and Happiness
Jenny Hulme
ISBN 978 1 78592 096 7
eISBN 978 1 78450 359 8

Games and Activities for Exploring Feelings with Children
Giving Children the Confidence to Navigate Emotions and Friendships
Vanessa Rogers
ISBN 978 1 84905 222 1
eISBN 978 0 85700 459 8

The Big Book of EVEN MORE Therapeutic
Activity Ideas for Children and Teens
Inspiring Arts-Based Activities and Character Education Curricula
Lindsey Joiner
ISBN 978 1 84905 749 3
eISBN 978 1 78450 196 9

Creating Excellence in Primary School Playtimes
How to Make 20% of the School Day 100% Better
Michael Follett
ISBN 978 1 78592 098 1
eISBN 978 1 78450 361 1

CHARACTER TOOLKIT FOR TEACHERS

100+ CLASSROOM AND WHOLE SCHOOL CHARACTER EDUCATION ACTIVITIES FOR 5- TO 11-YEAR-OLDS

FREDERIKA ROBERTS AND ELIZABETH WRIGHT

Foreword by Kristján Kristjánsson

Jessica Kingsley *Publishers*
London and Philadelphia

First published in 2018
by Jessica Kingsley Publishers
73 Collier Street
London N1 9BE, UK
and
400 Market Street, Suite 400
Philadelphia, PA 19106, USA

www.jkp.com

Library of Congress Cataloging in Publication Data
A CIP catalog record for this book is available from the Library of Congress

British Library Cataloguing in Publication Data
A CIP catalogue record for this book is available from the British Library

ISBN 978 1 78592 490 3
eISBN 978 1 78450 879 1

Printed and bound in the United States

Certified Chain of Custody
Promoting Sustainable Forestry
www.sfiprogram.org
SFI-01268

SFI label applies to the text stock

To Charlie and Hannah, whose character strengths shine like beacons, inspiring me every day to do better and be better.

Mamma (Frederika)

To Mum, who only ever simply wanted me to be happy. I want you to know that I am.

Elizabeth

Contents

Foreword

I am honoured to have been asked to write a few words to introduce this well-crafted and useful book.

Most parents and teachers believe that good character should ideally be *caught* (through the ethos of the school and the home) and *sought* (by young people themselves as they grow up to become teenagers and form their own moral identities). However, many people doubt that character can usefully be *taught* through specific classes, lessons or activities. They think that character education only works by osmosis.

This new book does a good job in dispelling these doubts and quelling the unease that some people have about exercises to 'instil' positive character traits. Frederika and Elizabeth show that, while the cultivation of character is no rocket science, it requires ingenuity and skill. The exercises have to be engaging and fun and they need to tap into children's developmental trajectories at their particular age levels. The authors come with a series of brilliant exercises and lesson plans: a true treasure trove of tools to inculcate positive character traits without indoctrination or undue paternalism.

What I particularly like about this book is how it aims to contribute to well-rounded character development by focusing on all four categories of character traits: *moral, civic, performative* and *intellectual*. Many teaching manuals about character only fore-ground performance skills such as grit, resilience, self-confidence and teamwork. As important as those are, mere excellence at such skills can be counter-productive from the point of view of the development of the whole person – for who would, for example, want to contribute to the resilience of the repeat offender? 'Good character' is an intrinsically normative concept, not just an instrumentalist one, and it requires ethical constraints.

While this book is essentially practical, the authors are clever at 'smuggling in' explicit or implicit responses to various possible misgivings, such as that the cultivation of character will always be relative to geographical or religious variances. Are there any places in the world, or any religions, where people are not eager to see their children become more grateful and kind? I very much doubt that; and – as Aristotle pointed out 2,300 years ago – the more we travel, the more we see how similar all human beings are deep down.

Frederika and Elizabeth are keenly aware of the fact that the cultivation of good character is not just about making children pliable and nice. Character formation is intimately connected to issues of mental and physical health. Some virtuous emotional traits – for example, gratitude and awe – have been shown to be closely related to better mental health and even lower levels of pro-inflammatory cytokines. No one knows yet exactly what the causal links are, but what matters is that each child is a holistic being where the flourishing of one developmental component is likely to be connected to the flourishing of others.

We therefore have good reason to believe that the successful implementation of the strategies explored and explained in this excellent book will be conducive to the overall flourishing of our children. For that reason I wholeheartedly recommend this work to anyone engaged in the crucial social practice of bringing up the next generation of human beings.

Kristján Kristjánsson
Professor of Character Education and Virtue Ethics
University of Birmingham, UK

Acknowledgements

They say it takes a village to raise a child; similarly, it takes a global community to write a book. First, we'd like to thank James, our brilliant editor at Jessica Kingsley Publishers, for sharing our vision for this book, being our champion right from the start and setting us the challenge of writing this book in just eight weeks! James has been invaluable in helping us make this book the best it can be, and has displayed admirable patience in answering our never-ending questions. We would also like to extend our thanks to the lovely Sean Townsend, who has supported James in supporting us. And of course, we'd like to thank the entire team at Jessica Kingsley Publishers for embracing our idea so wholeheartedly and supporting us every step of the way.

Before this book was even the seed of an idea, there was our 'RWS | Resilience Wellbeing Success' signature character and positive education programme, which has inspired us to write this book, so it's only right to acknowledge the many teachers and other education professionals who have helped us, and RWS, along the way. In no particular order, therefore, we would like to thank Kate Sowter, Hannah Wilson, Clare Erasmus, Kate Chisholm, Richard Rutter, Jamie Dillon, Ceri Stokes, Claire Russon, Lauren Knussen, Flora Barton, Mark Brotherton, Clive Rickart, Jill Howard, Katie Lawson, Maria O'Neill, Matt Young, Lee Jackson, Rebecca McGuinn, Louisa Simons, Tony Stephens and Fabian de Fabiani. We would also like to thank all the schools that have invited us to work with their pupils, staff and parents, and in particular the pilot schools that believed in us when RWS was just an idea in its infancy: Clifton with Rawcliffe, St Barnabas, Poppleton Road and St Clare's Primary Schools. We'd also like to extend our special thanks to our third founder member of RWS, Jayne Snell, with whom we worked closely as a friend and colleague for two years. Our heartfelt thanks also go to Sir Anthony Seldon, who kindly gave us his time and his advice at the inaugural International Positive Education Network (IPEN) Festival in Dallas, and introduced us to Kristján Kristjánsson, Professor of Character Education and Virtue Ethics and Deputy Director of the Jubilee Centre for Character and Virtues, which ultimately led to Elizabeth undertaking the MA in Character Education. We are hugely honoured and grateful that Kristján has written the brilliant foreword to this book.

Both of us are fortunate to have the support of some amazing academics as part of our studies, but also in making this book happen. At the Jubilee Centre for Character and Virtues, Tom Harrison has been an enthusiastic and invaluable supporter, as have Christian van Nieuwerburgh at the University of East London, formerly at Anglia Ruskin University (ARU), as well as Ilona Boniwell and Evie Rosset at ARU. While mentioning ARU, Frederika would like to particularly thank her amazing fellow 'MAPPsters' and especially the awesome 'PP Islanders', with a special mention of Muriel Boettger for supporting her and keeping her accountable so she could complete two university assignments to coincide with the manuscript deadline!

There is a reason why this book has a big chapter dedicated to relationships and connections: they matter. Our friends, families and professional contacts have been simply fantastic in supporting us, believing in us, and offering help in extending the reach of our book. We have been blessed to have the support of our 'Butterpillar' Mastermind group; David Abbott and Anthony Day's unwavering belief in us has been invaluable throughout the writing of this book. Through our work, we have been incredibly fortunate to attend some highly informative – and fun – international conferences, where we have met some wonderful practitioners and academics at the forefront of character and positive education. For their friendship and practical help in disseminating the book, we would like to thank, in no particular order, some of these fantastic human beings: Caren Baruch-Feldman, Jane Kirkham, Beverley Myatt and Mark Liston.

All of our friends and family have been unconditionally supportive and understanding during our writing of this book. Frederika would especially like to thank her husband Simon and her daughters Charlie and Hannah for their unwavering patience throughout the writing process, as well as her mum and sister for giving her little moral boosts when she needed them. Also, Frederika and Elizabeth may not have got through the final week without Sue's mouthwatering carrot cake! Elizabeth would like to especially thank her dad, who has always believed in her, no matter what crazy stuff she decides to do, as well as her friends Anj and Jess, who have been her cheerleaders throughout this process.

To everyone we have listed above, and everyone we couldn't fit into this book, we'd like to extend our deepest gratitude for your help, support and belief in us. With your help, we hope this book will help teachers all over the world improve the lives of the children they work with.

INTRODUCTION

You know that boy who can't sit still for one minute and focus on school work? How amazing would it be to see him sitting and quietly meditating for three minutes? How priceless would the look on his face be at the end, as he lights up with pride at his achievement? Or what about that girl whose grandad is ill and who as a result of a character workshop is now able to identify *hope* as her strongest character trait? Or the girl who tells you she now suffers fewer panic attacks as a result of her work on gratitude? Character and positive psychology work with children (and adults!) can be transformative. That's why we do the work we do, and probably why you picked up this book! Until we launched our character and positive education programme in 2015, we didn't realise just how powerful this work could be, but the examples above are real; we experienced these with pupils who had gone through our programme.

Our experience of working in schools highlighted to us that there is a big gap between what teachers want to achieve for their pupils, and what the traditional curriculum allows them time for. Additionally, children's and adolescents' mental health is a growing concern worldwide (Costello *et al.* 2003; Farbstein *et al.* 2010; Public Health England 2017; World Health Organization 2005). Equipping children with essential skills to look after their mental health is increasingly important, because we have a collective responsibility to look after the wellbeing of the whole child, and because studies have linked the *subjective wellbeing* of students with 'academic functioning, social competence, physical health, achievements and behavioural engagement in school' (Antaramian *et al.* 2010, as cited in Shoshani and Steinmetz 2014, pp.1290–1).

This is why we developed a comprehensive character and positive education programme 'RWS | Resilience Wellbeing Success',[1] supported by teacher training and development (In-Service Training/Continuing Professional Development) workshops, as well as information workshops for parents, to help schools provide character and positive education to their children, without impacting on the workload of their teachers. We also realise, however, that it is not always possible for schools to implement a full programme; an activities toolkit allows those schools to bring character and positive education into their lessons and school culture. Schools that already run character and positive education programmes can also benefit from additional activities they can run in order to keep the momentum going and firmly embed the principles in their classrooms and into the school-wide culture.

We understand that you don't have the time to wade through hundreds of pages of theory. This is why we wanted to write a book that offers practical, immediately accessible activities you can use in the classroom and within the whole school. Our aim is for this book to make your life easier. Chances are, you know the *why*. This book offers you the *how*.

What are character education and positive education?

Character and positive education are two distinct yet intrinsically linked schools of thought that focus on how to best educate the whole child, beyond the purely academic curriculum. For this reason, we have included them as two separate sections in this book, but you will find that we have cross-referenced activities between the two sections as there is so much commonality of purpose.

---

1   www.rws.today

Character is made up of the unique traits that define a person: their strengths, personal values and behaviours. Character education helps children discover their unique traits and develop an understanding of how to use them in everyday life to benefit them and the wider community around them. Positive education is the application of positive psychology research to educational settings to facilitate flourishing and increase happiness and wellbeing. Many researchers straddle both character and positive education, and bring perspectives from psychology (including cognitive, social and educational), sociology, anthropology, philosophy and many more into this growing field. Peterson and Seligman's *Character Strengths and Virtues* (2004) 'was hailed as the "backbone of Positive Psychology"' (VIA Institute on Character n.d.) when it was first published; thus both areas have been interconnected for quite some time. It therefore only seems right to start this book with a section on character education, followed by a section on positive education.

Are character education and positive education limited to one country or region?

As we have mentioned, welbeing and flourishing lie at the heart of character and positive education. The *Penn Resiliency Program* (PRP), which was launched in the USA and has been running worldwide since the 1990s, addresses these. Seligman *et al.* (2009) reference research that has evaluated PRP's effectiveness in children and adolescents aged 8–15 years: 'PRP studies include adolescents from a variety of racial/ethnic backgrounds, community settings (urban, suburban and rural) and countries (e.g. United States, United Kingdom, Australia, China and Portugal)' (p.297).

Why do character education and positive education matter?

Character education is nothing new; it has been around for thousands of years, going back to ancient philosophers in all corners of the world. In the second half of the 20th century, character education fell out of favour, with an increased focus on academic disciplines (Jubilee Centre for Character and Virtues 2017; Shlain and The Moxie Institute 2017). Around 30 years later, at the start of the 21st century, academics and politicians started to look at character education again. There is now a growing body of evidence supporting the view that character education improves academic attainment (Arthur and O'Shaugnessy 2012). The benefits of character education reach beyond academic attainment, helping pupils make moral distinctions between behaviour choices, improving their overall wellbeing, and helping them flourish. For more information, see also the introduction to Section 1, 'Character Education', in the present book. Currently, 97 per cent of schools in the UK seek to develop character traits in their pupils, but only over half of them understand what character education means (Department for Education 2017). This book aims to change that.

Whilst positive psychology is often associated with individual happiness, from its initial roots (Sheldon *et al.* 2000), there has also always been a focus on the improvement of child education and the flourishing of families, workplaces and society as a whole. Positive education reflects this in a school setting, both through specific interventions and as an educational ethos. Seligman *et al.* (2009) describe positive education interventions as ones that develop academic skills and wellbeing side-by-side. Shoshani and Steinmetz (2014) provide examples from Geelong Grammar School in Australia and Strath Haven High School in the USA, where positive psychology interventions resulted in increased flourishing of individuals, more successful student conflict resolution, increased engagement in and enjoyment of school, and better social skills.

The IPEN[2] links character, positive education (described as wellbeing) and academic learning through their 'double helix' formula. This formula can be applied beyond the scope of the

---

2   www.ipen-network.com/about

classroom to commercial and non-profit organisations, government, and the wider community.

Whole school and cross-curricular approach

Each chapter includes suggested whole school activities. Whatever initiatives you decide to trial/implement, it is important that the entire school community knows about the initiative and understands its purpose, to ensure maximum participation and benefit. Also, remember not to get carried away by enthusiasm, and risk *initiative overload* by introducing lots of initiatives all at once!

Introducing, or extending the range of, character and positive education activities in the classroom and school-wide should not feel like a bolt-on or a chore. In fact, it is possible to integrate many character and positive education activities into other subjects. In their review of positive psychology classroom interventions, Seligman *et al.* (2009, p.305) give a number of examples from Geelong Grammar School in Australia, such as using character strengths to assist in discussing the content of books as part of the English Language curriculum, incorporating discussions about pleasure and ethics within the Religious Education curriculum, and changing the language used in school, from focusing on negatives (e.g. 'give a speech on a time you were embarrassed or made a fool out of yourself') to positives (e.g. 'give a speech about when you were of value to others'). The Jubilee Centre for Character and Virtues produced a research report (Arthur *et al.* 2014a) into the integration of character across the curriculum, showing that this is possible in a number of subjects and works particularly well in literacy. From time to time, where we feel an activity lends itself particularly well to a cross-curricular application, we have mentioned this along with the description of the activity in this book.

One aspect of the whole school impact of character and positive education that should not be overlooked is its impact on teachers. We have found that teaching character and positive psychology interventions has a positive impact on our own wellbeing. We come out of our workshops buzzing and wondering, 'Should work really feel this great?!' Of course, even as experienced practitioners in this field, we occasionally forget to practise what we preach, but doing the work we do gives us regular nudges (Halpern 2016) and keeps us on the straight and narrow! This book can be your nudge. By using these activities with your pupils, you will reap the benefits as well, and of course you can use the interventions on yourself and your family, too – many teachers tell us they do.

We hope that this book will help you seamlessly integrate character and positive education activities into your curriculum and expand the ways in which your school focuses on the education of the whole child. We firmly believe that schools have a vital role to fulfil in the broader education of children, ensuring they are fully equipped to function in our complex world, so they can flourish in all aspects of their lives.

HOW TO USE
THIS BOOK

In each chapter we will touch on the theories and research behind the interventions, with pointers for you to find more information if you want it, but the main focus of the book is on practical activities, with clear instructions and timings. All the activities are based on validated character education and positive psychology research and interventions.

You can, of course, read this book from cover to cover, starting with Chapter 1 and working your way through. This method may give you a good overview of the suggested activities and prompt ideas for fitting these into your curriculum for the year, as well as for bringing character and positive education into the whole school culture and ethos. The book is, however, designed to allow you to dip in and out of it, choosing activities based on particular character traits you wish to work on with your pupils, or positive psychology interventions you are particularly interested in undertaking. This means that, with minimal time commitment, you can simply pick up the book and choose an activity from any chapter.

Although the book is generally intended for use by teachers of 5- to 11-year-old children, it includes activities that work with older children. This also allows for children's individual differences in emotional and academic development. For each activity, we have shown suggested ages as follows:

- A range of ages (e.g. 8–11)

- A starting age (e.g. 8+), meaning that there is no upper limit and the activity would work with older children, teenagers, and adults.

Throughout the book, we often refer to the 24 VIA Character Strengths. These are explained in the introduction to Section 1, 'Character Education'. We invite you to refer back to those pages whenever an activity mentions the VIA Character Strengths.

CHARACTER EDUCATION

Character education is a broad subject spanning philosophical, psychological, sociological and educational thought. Across the world, educational institutions and academic researchers are exploring what character means and how we can apply it successfully to help our young people lead flourishing lives. In the USA the focus is mainly on the psychological perspective, whereas in the UK the research focus is more philosophical and sociological.

The Jubilee Centre for Character and Virtues (2017) describes character as 'a set of personal traits or dispositions that produce specific moral emotions, inform motivation and guide conduct' (p.2). Character education, therefore, is influenced by the culture and communities we live in, and the institutions guiding our ethics (Jubilee Centre for Character and Virtues 2017). Research by the Jubilee Centre shows that when character education is actively embedded in the school curriculum, pupils' behaviour can improve, and their ability to apply *practical wisdom* (the ability to judge the right action/thought at the right moment) develops (Arthur *et al.* 2014a).

Much research has been undertaken into character strengths and the impact these can have on wellbeing and success. In 2004, Peterson and Seligman developed a classification of 24 universal character traits that led to the development of the VIA Institute on Character. A list of the 24 VIA Character Strengths, and their descriptions, can be found on the VIA website.[1] Biswas-Diener (2006) carried out further research across three vastly different cultures and geographical locations, showing that in all those cultures, people recognise the existence and importance of the VIA Character Strengths, and believe they can be developed. There was some variability between cultures in terms of the importance of individual traits, but there was general agreement that helping young people develop character strengths is a worthwhile pursuit.

Working on and with our character strengths can have a positive impact on our behaviour, our thought processes, our self-esteem and overall wellbeing. Understanding not only our own strengths but also those of others can improve relationships with our closest family and friends, our peers and the wider community. Recent criticism of character education points to the dominance of performance character strengths, such as grit, perseverance and leadership in schools. These are, of course, important traits, but not on their own. Moral and civic character strengths (e.g. kindness and gratitude) need to be developed alongside them.

In this section, we will focus on character strengths that enhance wellbeing and academic attainment, and hold moral and civic value.

---

1 www.viacharacter.org

∗ Chapter 1 ∗

GRATITUDE

Gratitude is both an emotion and a character trait. It is a positive emotion we experience spontaneously, sometimes overwhelmingly, when something good happens. It can be mixed with relief (e.g. when a negative outcome is averted). Based on Fredrickson's research (Fredrickson 2001) – please also refer to Chapter 6, 'Happiness and Positive Emotions' – it is a good idea to deliberately increase the ratio of positive emotions, such as gratitude, to negative ones, in order to increase resilience and wellbeing.

As a character trait, gratitude is one of the VIA Character Strengths,[1] so whether you have it by the bucket load or it's a trait you display more reticently, you do have the capacity to feel and express gratitude. Research (Seligman *et al.* 2005) shows that carrying out specific gratitude activities can improve happiness and reduce symptoms of depression. In a study by Froh *et al.* (2008, as cited in Shoshani and Steinmetz 2014), *subjective wellbeing* showed increased levels three weeks after adolescents in middle school had carried out an exercise listing five daily gratitudes. There was also a significant relationship between gratitude and the students' satisfaction with school, immediately after the intervention and three weeks later.

It is important to recognise that, sometimes, gratitude can include negative emotions, such as feeling indebted to someone, feeling a sense of obligation or guilt, and even awkwardness or

---

1   www.viacharacter.org

embarrassment (Morgan, Gulliford and Kristjánsson 2014). Morgan *et al.* found this to be more prevalent in the UK than the USA, so there are potentially cultural differences that need to be taken into account when introducing gratitude activities. If one of your pupils experiences such negative emotions when practising gratitude, acknowledge the feelings and reassure them it's OK to feel that way. Encourage them to stick with it if they can. Tell them if they still don't like it after they've given it a proper chance, they don't have to keep doing it, but like many new activities or situations, sometimes it just takes an open mind and a bit of time to get used to it.

Different forms of gratitude

You can feel gratitude for a number of reasons:

- You might be grateful to a professional person (e.g. a doctor, a nurse, a teacher) when they have helped you as part of their job. People are often grateful when such a person is 'just doing their job', but tend to be particularly grateful when that person has 'gone the extra mile' for them.

- You can be grateful to people you've never met, when what they did has an impact years later (e.g. when we remember fallen soldiers, we are grateful that they gave their lives for our freedom and safety; or we may be grateful to past political figures or activists for having created long-lasting change and improvement in society).

- You can also feel gratitude that isn't directed towards a specific person, but is rather a wider appreciation of circumstances or events, such as the beauty of nature itself or a glorious rainbow on a rainy day.

- Although we usually focus our gratitude on positive events, it is also possible to be grateful for negative events (e.g. because of how they've made us stronger or because of what we have learnt from them). Gratitude can therefore be incredibly powerful in overcoming difficulties in life.

Will it always work?

It isn't entirely clear when children start to truly feel and express gratitude, but it appears to begin somewhere between the ages of 6 and 8 years (Froh, Miller and Snyder 2007). Most of our activities are therefore aimed at this age group and above. For some of the activities, however, we have indicated an earlier age, as a simple introduction to the concept.

Not all children are ready to practise gratitude at the same age, so as with all the activities in this book, we recommend you use your judgement and knowledge of the children you work with. To help children with the activities, give them examples from your own experience wherever possible, before asking them to come up with their own ideas.

If a child struggles to think of gratitudes, try to refocus them onto things that have gone well that day, or things they enjoyed, or things that made them smile or laugh, for example.

When it comes to expressing gratitude to specific people, you may get the occasional 'I can't think of anyone to thank for anything' response. If so, gently ask the child to talk you through their day/last couple of days: *What did they eat, for example? Who cooked their food? Did they laugh at any point in the day? Who did or said something funny?* This should, in most instances, help them think of someone to thank, but if it doesn't, don't push the point. Give them something else to do (perhaps choose an activity from a different chapter in this book) and allow them to come around to gratitude in their own time.

▦ 1.1 THREE GOOD THINGS ▦▦▦▦▦

This is one of the activities researched by Seligman et al. (2005). You can hear Martin Seligman talk about it in a YouTube video (Happierdotcom and Seligman 2009). At the end of each day, for seven days, write down 'three good things' (Seligman et al. 2005, p.416) about your day and the cause for each. The research has shown that doing this, especially if you keep going for longer than seven days (and we hope you will want to carry on after the first seven days because you will feel great!), can increase happiness and reduce symptoms of depression for up to six months. Seligman et al. (2009) also used this activity as part of a whole school positive psychology intervention at Geelong Grammar School in Australia. They asked pupils to write down 'three good things' each day for a week, followed up by a reflection on one question out of three. The questions invited pupils to explore why the good thing happened, how they could make it more likely that more instances of it would happen in future, and what it meant to them.

1.1.1 Gratitude diary in lesson time

- Recommended age

  8+

- Duration

  5–10 minutes per day

- Resources

  » Exercise books (one per pupil)

  » Pens/pencils

- Method

  Set aside time during lessons for pupils to write down three things that went well that day (if done at the end of the school day), or three things that went well the previous day (if done at the start of the school day).

  Explain the activity to pupils. Below is some suggested wording:

  You will keep a 'Gratitude Diary' for seven days. Did you know that if you write down three things that went well each day, for seven days, and also write down why those things happened, you are likely to feel happier?

For each day, write down three good things about your day (for example, something good that happened, or something you saw that made you feel happy), and for each one, write why you think it happened, or why you are grateful for that thing.

For example: 'I am grateful that I got a good grade in my test today, because I worked hard for it. I am grateful that Paul joined our school today, because I think he will become my best friend. I am grateful that I didn't get cold outside today, because I was wearing my coat.'

On our website (Roberts 2017a), you can read our case study about a school where the Year 5 teacher kept this activity going for a full academic year. As you will see from the example gratitudes displayed, children tended to focus on generic life gratitudes rather than specific things that had gone well on any given day. This did not detract from the overall positive impact of the activity, though was possibly a cause for the children's occasional boredom with gratitude journalling.

▨ 1.1.2 Gratitude diary as homework

- **Recommended age**

  8+

- **Duration**

  5–10 minutes per day (homework)

- **Resources**

  » Exercise books (one per pupil)

  » Pens/pencils

- **Method**

Follow the same method as for the 'Gratitude diary in lesson time' activity, but set this as homework instead, encouraging children to take responsibility for their gratitude diaries.

It would be useful to explain the activity and its purpose to parents, so that they can support and encourage their children in its daily completion.

1.1.3 Daily class gratitudes

- **Recommended age**

5–11

- **Duration**

5–10 minutes per day

- **Resources**

  » None required, unless you wish to keep a record of the gratitudes, perhaps for a display

- **Method**

At the end of each school day, ask the whole class if anyone wants to share one good thing that happened to them, or that they noticed that day.

To ensure this doesn't become a hugely time-consuming activity, you can explain to the class that you will allow three people to share one good thing each, every day, or you can allocate a set time to this activity and hear as many good things as you can fit into the time. Encourage children to share their gratitudes with their families, too.

◼ 1.1.4 Gratitude beach ball display

● **Recommended age**

5–11

● **Duration**

10 minutes per day

● **Resources**

» Paper and pens for children to draw an outline of a beach ball, or paper with an outline of a beach ball already on it (one per child). Each beach ball needs to have six segments plus a centre circle, so children will have seven spaces to write/draw on. You can easily find these by doing an online clipart search.

» Felt-tip pens, wax crayons or coloured pencils for children to write/draw on the beach balls and to colour them in at the end of the seven days

» Pens

» Scissors

» A space (e.g. a wall in a corridor or in the classroom) to display the completed gratitude beach balls

● **Method**

This is a variation aimed at younger children, or children who may find the full written activity too challenging. It is also a beautiful and colourful way to display gratitude in school as a constant reminder to practise this character trait and positive emotion.

In our workshops, we find that beach balls are a great way to illustrate resilience as 'bounce-back ability'. You can do this with your pupils, explaining how the air in the beach ball is the resilience that keeps you bouncing back after each difficulty or challenge in life, and that being grateful for the big and little things is one way to put more air into the beach ball.

Once you have supplied the paper with beach ball outlines to your pupils, or they have drawn their own, give your class the following instruction:

Each day, starting today, write or draw three things you are grateful for in one segment of the beach ball. For example, you may be grateful that your best friend is coming to play at your house after school today, or that your mum is cooking your favourite food tonight. There are seven segments in the ball, including the circle, so you need to write down your gratitudes for seven days. You can colour in the ball to make it look bright and exciting. After seven days, you will cut the ball out and we will create a class display with everyone's colourful beach balls.

1.2 GRATITUDE LETTER

This is based on Martin Seligman's 'Gratitude Visit' (Seligman et al. 2005, p.416) activity, where participants were given a week to write a letter to someone who had been particularly kind to them but whom they had never thanked, and then to deliver the letter. This exercise caused large positive changes for one month.

1.2.1 Gratitude letter – class or homework activity

* **Recommended age**

  10+

* **Duration**

  30 minutes

- **Resources**

  » Draft paper and good-quality paper

  » Pens

- **Method**

  Set sufficient time aside in class for this activity (it could be spread over more than one day – for example, time in one lesson for drafting, and time in a subsequent lesson for neat writing up/ decorating with drawings), or set it as a homework activity.

  It would be useful to inform parents about this activity, as their co-operation would help in the second part of the activity: 'Delivering the letters'.

  Give your pupils the following instruction:

  Take some time to think about a person who has done something for you that you feel grateful for. Write that person a 'Thank you' letter, explaining in detail what they did, why it was important to you, and the positive impact their actions had on you. Thank them for what they did.

  If you can, deliver the letter in person. You may wish to read it out to them or sit with them while they read it, but just delivering it and putting it in their hands will be great. If you can't deliver it in person (maybe the person doesn't live near you), you can post the letter instead, or read it out to them over the phone.

  You may want to write a gratitude letter to a person who is no longer alive, and that is fine, too.

  Research has shown that writing a gratitude letter can improve your happiness for up to a month, so try to write a gratitude letter once a month.

  Why not write a gratitude letter to yourself, too, from time to time?

▦ 1.2.2 Gratitude drawing

- **Recommended age**

  5–11

- **Duration**

  20 minutes

- **Resources**

  » Paper for pupils to draw on

  » Coloured pencils, felt-tip pens, coloured crayons for children to draw with

- **Method**

  Provide pupils with appropriate paper and pens/crayons, etc. for them to draw their pictures. Give them the following instruction:

  Draw a picture to say 'Thank you'. For example, you could thank your parents for looking after you, or your friend for making you laugh. There are probably lots of people who do nice things for you. Who do you want to thank and what for?

▦ 1.2.3 'Thank you' card

This activity works as a stand-alone, or you can combine it with the 'Gratitude drawing' activity above, in which case, you will need to ensure the drawings are small enough to cut and glue onto a folded card, or are drawn directly onto an appropriately sized folded piece of card.

- **Recommended age**

  7+

- **Duration**

  20 minutes

- **Resources**

  » Existing pupil drawings from the 'Gratitude drawing' activity (if you are doing this as two combined but separate activities)

  » Card for pupils to fold in half (either A4 for a large A5-size folded card, or A5 for an A6-size folded card)

  » Coloured pencils, felt-tip pens, coloured crayons (if not using previously created drawings)

  » Glue (if sticking previous 'Gratitude drawings' onto the front of the card)

  » Pens

- **Method**

  Option 1: Convert the existing 'Gratitude drawings' into a card

  Explain to your pupils that they will now convert their previous 'Gratitude drawings' into a 'Thank you' card.

  Provide them with the card and instruct them to fold it in half, then ask them to glue their previous drawings on the front. Then tell your pupils to write a 'Thank you' message inside the card, ensuring they address it to the appropriate person (e.g. 'Dear...', 'To...'), with a brief message explaining what they are grateful for and why, and signing it with their name and appropriate sign-off (e.g. 'Lots of love...', 'With love...', 'From...').

  Option 2: Draw directly onto card

  This activity is the same as Option 1, except for the drawing element, which children will do directly on the front of the card.

▨ 1.3 OTHER GRATITUDE ACTIVITIES ▨▨▨▨

▨ 1.3.1 Musical beach ball gratitudes

This is an activity we run in all our 'Resilience' workshops as part of the 'RWS | Resilience Wellbeing Success'[2] signature programme. By around age 10–11, children become a little bit more self-conscious about the dancing element, but most really enjoy writing gratitudes on the beach balls. Interestingly, 'school' features at least once on every occasion we do this!

- Recommended age

  7–10

- Duration

  5–10 minutes

- Resources

  » Large inflatable panel beach balls (one per five children)

  » Colourful permanent markers/felt-tip pens that will write on the beach balls

  » Uplifting song/music that children are likely to know and recognise and can dance to

- Method

  As with the 'Gratitude beach ball display' drawing/writing activity (1.1.4), explain to the children how the air in the beach ball is the resilience that keeps you bouncing back after each difficulty or challenge in life, and that being grateful for the big and little things is one way to put more air into the beach ball.

  Tell them how the activity will run:

---

2   www.rws.today

1. *Children collect a pen each* [or there are some 'central' stocks of pens on various tables].

2. *Teacher will start the music.*

3. *Teacher will throw the beach balls into the room.*

4. *Whoever catches a beach ball needs to quickly write one thing they are grateful for (or one good thing about their day, something that made them smile, etc.) on the beach ball, then throw it back into the room to give another pupil a chance to write. When children don't have a beach ball, they can dance (and sing, if they like) to the music, while thinking about what gratitude they want to write on the ball when they get it.*

5. *When the music stops, whoever has a ball brings it back to the front of the class, and everyone puts the pens back.*

Play the music, throw the balls in, and have fun dancing with the children!

1.3.2 Gratitude chain links

This is an adaptation that one of the teaching assistants we worked with[3] came up with to use in her school. She found it worked very well.

● **Recommended age**

5–11

● **Duration**

20 minutes

---

3   www.rws.today/coaching-consultation-programme-teaching-assistants-case-study

- **Resources**

  » Strips of colourful paper (big enough to write on, small enough to loop into circles and form a chain with other strips of paper)

  » Felt-tip pens/wax crayons/coloured pencils

  » Glue

  » Something to stick the ends of the chain to the wall/ceiling with (e.g. pins, staples)

- **Method**

  Explain to the children that you will make colourful chains to display in the classroom, full of gratitudes.

  Give each child an equal number of strips of paper, and ask them to write a gratitude or 'good thing' about their day on each one, leaving enough room at each end to overlap and glue the ends together to form a link in the chain.

  Work as a class team to create the chain – glue the ends of the first strip of paper together to make the first chain link, then loop the next piece of paper through the link before applying glue to the ends to form the next link, and so on.

  Hang the chain from a wall or across the ceiling as a reminder of all the gratitudes.

▦ 1.4 WHOLE SCHOOL ACTIVITIES ▦▦▦▦▦

How can we promote the gratitude character trait in school overall, thereby also increasing the amount of positive emotions that pupils and staff feel? This is something you could discuss at a Senior Leadership Team or staff meeting, or of course do as a brainstorming activity with your class. Your pupils are bound to come up with some fantastic and innovative suggestions! Some of ours are on the next page.

1.4.1 School gratitude board

Make space available for a gratitude display in a prominent location in school – for example, near the entrance, where parents and visitors will also see it, or in a high-traffic corridor.

Prepare the space as appropriate with backing paper/card if needed.

Provide small, colourful pieces of paper for pupils and staff to use to write down their gratitudes. You will need to ensure everyone in school understands this initiative and that they know where to obtain the small pieces of paper and where to hand them in. It would help to have a person responsible for collecting the gratitudes and displaying them on the board.

Encourage pupils and staff to write down gratitudes whenever they feel like it (the more, the better!), whether they are generic ones about aspects of their lives, good things they have noticed, or specific gratitudes to individual people within or outside school.

1.4.2 Unsung hero awards

Create or buy a box for people to post their gratitudes (specifically directed at pupils or staff in school, naming the person they are grateful to and what they have done to warrant that gratitude).

Create some gratitude nomination sheets (these could perhaps be A5-sized, to allow enough space for a brief description to be written on). It would help to have some simple headings, based on the following:

» *Who do you want to thank?*

» *If it is a pupil, please write which class they are in.*

» *Why do you want to thank this person? Please give as much information as possible about what they did (either for you or for someone else) that you feel they need to be recognised for.*

» *You can remain anonymous if you wish, but if not, please write your name here.*

Decide how often (e.g. weekly, monthly) you are going to select an 'unsung hero' from the box, and how that selection will be done (e.g. a random draw, a 'gratitude committee') and how the winner will be announced (e.g. assembly, newsletter). Also decide what you will do about the remaining nominations. It may be more motivational and uplifting to celebrate them all, by collating them in a newsletter or reading them out in assembly, for example.

1.4.3 Gratitude email

Ask all staff to start their first email of the day, regardless of whether they are writing it to someone internally or externally, with a gratitude. For example, they could start an email to a colleague by writing 'Thank you for your warm smile this morning when you came in', or to a supplier with 'Thank you for always answering my queries so promptly', etc.

If all staff can develop this habit, school staff, parents, suppliers and other external stakeholders will all receive gratitudes in emails. In addition to fostering a spirit of gratitude within the school, word will soon spread about this, which can improve the reputation of the school, as well as create a ripple effect where parents, governors, suppliers and other people emailing the school also start their emails by expressing gratitudes. This could vastly improve relationships within and outside the school.

* Chapter 2 *

KINDNESS

We can probably all agree that it is morally good for human beings to be kind towards each other, but kindness offers benefits beyond its moral value. It increases happiness (Lyubomirsky, Sheldon and Schkade 2005), and creating a kindness culture in schools has been shown to reduce the negative impact of bullying (Clark and Marinak 2012). Being good makes us feel good. People often talk of the 'warm glow' they feel when they do something good. Seligman *et al.* (2009) give a lovely example of this: a class of 10- to 11-year-old children had undertaken a project whereby they learnt to make bread, which they then took to a nursing home. When the teacher asked the children whether it bothered them to give away the food they'd spent a long time preparing, one child declared that 'doing something for others felt better than any video game' (p.307).

What causes this 'feel-good factor'? Humans are social beings; caring for others has helped our species survive thus far. Our need to care, however, runs deeper than evolution. According to Lieberman (2015), it is 'part of our basic wiring' (p.84); for example, research has shown that our brain's *reward* centre is activated when we help others by giving money. Lieberman (2015) also talks about the importance of *oxytocin* – the hormone whose main purpose is to assist in childbirth and breastfeeding – in making us care for our babies and minimising our own suffering when helping someone who is suffering. Although oxytocin is often referred to as the 'love drug' or 'trust hormone', he prefers to call it the 'nurse neuropeptide' (p.93), because when nurses do their job, there is no love or trust there, but they are driven by a desire to help. As an interesting aside, oxytocin makes us care about our in-group members and strangers, but makes us hostile to members of out-groups we dislike (see the 'Will it always work?' section of Chapter 9, 'Positive Relationships'), for an explanation of in- and out-groups). As human beings, we are capable of harming others in many ways, so it is useful to encourage kindness in children as each act of kindness positively reinforces the behaviour through the experience of the feel-good effect.

Another reason for teaching children to be kind is the *norm of self-interest* (Miller 1999), which reflects a widespread belief in Western cultures that, as human beings, we are inherently self-interested. This becomes a self-fulfilling prophecy: we expect people to behave with only their own interests at heart, so we put in place measures (security measures, distrust, clauses in contracts, etc.) based on this expectation, which people then live up to. Also because of this belief that we are all self-interested, we 'don't want to appear to be boasting or come off as goody-two-shoes' (Lieberman 2015, p.97) when we do good, so we downplay our accounts of our good actions, which of course further feeds the societal belief that people are self-interested, and the circle self-perpetuates. It is therefore important to teach children that kindness is both part of our natural disposition as human beings, and socially acceptable. As Lieberman goes on to say:

> Just imagine what things would look like if we were taught about this in school and we understood that altruistic helping is just as natural as being selfish. The strange stigma associated with altruistic behaviour would be lifted, perhaps engendering far more prosocial behaviour. (Lieberman 2015, p.98)

Will it always work?

Trying to force a child to be kind is likely to create anything but the lovely warm feeling we get when we do something good. Enforced kindness is a chore likely to create resentment and anger, which the child could later associate with doing good deeds. It is always possible that a child does not want to participate in kindness activities, and we would not recommend forcing the issue. There are, however, things you can do to gently encourage the child, such as enquiring as to why they don't wish to participate, to gain an understanding of the underlying emotions. It can also be useful to ask a child about a time when someone has been kind to them, and what that felt like; then if they say it felt good, gently ask them whether they'd like to make someone else feel like that. There are, unfortunately, children who have experienced very little kindness themselves and who may feel uncomfortable when they are the recipients of an act of kindness and therefore don't see the value in being kind to others. In these cases, as in the case of a child who simply does not feel in the mood to be kind to others, it can be useful to direct them towards one of the 'Kindness to Self' activities (2.2). On the other hand, some children are great at being kind to others, but not so much to themselves. The self-kindness activities we have included are designed to incorporate an element of imagining they are a friend giving them advice, which may make this easier. If it is still an issue, consider working on their emotions first (see Chapter 6).

2.1 KINDNESS TOWARDS OTHER INDIVIDUALS

2.1.1 Help!

- **Recommended age**

  8+

- **Duration**

  10 minutes at the start of the week, 10 minutes after 7 days

- **Resources**
  - » Paper
  - » Pens

- **Method**
  Split your class into smaller groups of a suitable size for small group discussions. Ask pupils to discuss, in their small groups, as many ways as possible that they can help others over the course of the next week. You may wish to give them examples, such as tidying their room, helping a sibling with homework, being nice to a friend who is sad.

  Once pupils have discussed potential ways to help others, ask each child to choose one of the options they have come up with and do it every day for a week.

  After seven days, split the pupils into pairs and ask them to tell each other how helping someone made them feel.

2.1.2 Kindness feedback

This activity can be used as a stand-alone or as a more in-depth follow-up to the 'Help!' activity (2.1.1).

- **Recommended age**

  8+

- **Duration**

  20 minutes

- **Resources**
  - » Paper
  - » Pens
  - » Handout with questions if you choose to give them out rather than write/display them on the board

- **Method**

Either write the following questions on the board, or give them to pupils as a handout, and ask them to write down the answers:

1. *What is the kindest thing you have done for someone?*

2. *How did it make you feel?*

3. *Was there a reason why you wanted to be kind to that person (e.g. were they sad, did you want to show them you love them, did you want to say thank you for something)?*

4. *Did you plan the act of kindness, or was it something you decided on the spur of the moment?*

5. *How did this person react to your kindness?*

6. *What is the kindest thing someone else has done for you?*

7. *How did it make you feel?*

To either extend or modify this activity, you can also ask pupils to write the answers as a story and/or to draw pictures.

2.1.3 Kindness vouchers

This activity is great to do around celebrations when giving gifts is customary, such as birthdays or religious holidays, but can also be done at any time of the year. Pupils can give the resulting vouchers to a friend or family member for their birthday, or 'just because'. There really doesn't need to be a reason to be kind. Children will produce booklets of ten 'kindness vouchers' to give to someone as a gift, which that person can redeem whenever they wish.

- **Recommended age**

5–11

- **Duration**

30 minutes

- **Resources**

  » Paper (this could be pre-marked with rectangles to cut out to make the vouchers, or children could draw the rectangles themselves)

  » Coloured pens/pencils/crayons

  » Scissors

  » Pens

  » Stapler

- **Method**

  Explain to pupils that they will produce a 'kindness voucher' booklet to give to someone as a gift. The booklet will contain ten acts of kindness, which the person receiving the booklet can then redeem at any time.

  Give pupils ten minutes in groups to discuss:

  » Who might they want to give a booklet of 'kindness vouchers' to?

  » What acts of kindness could go in there? You could give them examples, such as a hug, reading a book together, clearing the table, telling a joke, singing a song, being nice to siblings (peaceful mealtimes!), etc.

  Armed with a list of acts of kindness, each child now works independently to create the booklet of vouchers:

  1. They need to cut out the voucher rectangles. They will need 11 rectangles for 10 vouchers and 1 cover sheet. They can either cut along the pre-drawn rectangles on the sheets you have provided, or you can build in a little bit of geometry work and get them to draw the rectangles themselves before cutting them out.

  2. Next, they need to write on each voucher what it is for.

3. They then colour in each voucher, and the cover sheet in whichever way they wish. They can write who the voucher booklet is for, and from, on the cover sheet.

4. Finally, they staple the vouchers together (possibly with your help, depending on the children's ages).

5. They take the vouchers home to give to whichever friend or family member they are for.

2.1.4 What would you do?

This activity is intended to get children to contemplate kind actions in the context of moral dilemmas. It can either be done as an individual written activity, or you can do it as a pairs or group discussion.

- **Recommended age**

  8–11

- **Duration**

  30 minutes

- **Resources**

  » Moral dilemmas and questions written on handouts or displayed on the board

  » Paper and pens (if this activity is done as a written activity)

- **Method**

  Provide pupils with the dilemma scenarios and questions below. Then either ask them to discuss the answers in pairs/groups (you circulate and facilitate the discussions), or to write the answers down.

  If you give them this exercise to do as a group discussion, you may wish to consider doing this as a 'Co-operative learning' exercise (see 9.1.6).

For each scenario, the questions are:

1. *What would you do?*

2. *Why?*

3. *What happens next?*

4. *How do you feel?*

Situation 1

Amy has just arrived at your school. She is new to the area as her family just moved here, so she doesn't know anyone. She has been in your class for a week and seems to be alone a lot. Your friends tell you she is 'a bit weird' and not interested in getting to know anyone. They say that she is rude if they speak to her. One lunchtime, you see her sitting in a corner of the playground, alone again.

Situation 2

Adam is a funny boy in your class. He always makes everyone laugh and tells lots of jokes. He often makes others laugh by being a bit naughty in lessons, answering back to the teacher with cheeky comments, giving deliberately wrong answers to questions and clowning around in PE.

You have all been given a project to work on at home for the past week and today you all presented your project back to the class. When it was Adam's turn, he made jokes and then, when the teacher insisted, Adam became quite angry, crossed his arms and refused to speak to the teacher.

During morning break, you see Adam coming out of the toilets with red eyes. It looks like he's been crying.

Situation 3

You have a new class teacher who has just joined the school to replace your previous teacher who has recently had a baby. Everybody loved the previous teacher and feels a little upset there is

*a new teacher to get used to. Because of this, some of the children in
your class are misbehaving in lessons, being rude or cheeky to the
teacher, not following instructions and talking when the teacher is
talking. At the end of the school day, they leave the classroom in a
mess, ignoring the teacher's requests to tidy up. After a couple of
days, as you leave school at the end of the day, you see the teacher
tidying up the classroom, looking very tired and a bit upset.*

2.1.5 Support circles

In this activity, children have the opportunity to ask for specific
help, and to offer help to those who need it.

- **Recommended age**

  8+

- **Duration**

  30–60 minutes

- **Resources**

  » Flipchart (and flipchart pens) or blackboard/whiteboard (and
  chalk/whiteboard pens)

- **Method**

  This activity can be done with a whole class, although it would work
  better with smaller groups, such as particular groups of children
  you might be working with outside of a classroom setting. It is
  essential to set some ground rules before starting this activity for
  the first time, and to reiterate the agreed ground rules before each
  further session. (See our 'Class rules' activity, 9.1.5, for a suggested
  way of doing this.)

  Each child has the opportunity to ask for help with something
  (children who don't want help with anything can still participate
  as the real benefit of the activity lies in the giving, rather than the

receiving, of help). They may have difficulty with some school work, or may wish to discuss a more emotive issue that they want advice on, or some practical question they need help with.

As you listen to each child's request for help, write this down on the flipchart or board. Once everyone who wants help has said what they want help with, the class votes on which items to discuss together. There are a couple of ways you can do the voting:

» Each child nominates one activity they wish to discuss/help with (it can't be their own!), and the activities with the most nominations are the ones you discuss.

» You read out each item on the list and have a show of hands (children can't vote for their own!) for how many children want to discuss/help with each one. The activities with the most votes are the ones you discuss.

We recommend allowing 10–30 minutes per topic, depending on the age and maturity of the children, and the complexity of the issues they have raised. Ensure you allocate equal time, and tell children beforehand how many activities they will discuss. You can also decide whether some of the requests for help need to be addressed in a future group session, or can be addressed in a different way individually. This is something that could be agreed in the ground rules before you start.

You then proceed to discuss solutions to each of the selected problems for the allocated time per problem. Your role is mainly that of a facilitator, ensuring that children stay focused on the topic and that the conversation is constructive and meaningful. With larger groups, you may wish to split the children into smaller sub-groups to discuss and then bring them back together to share their answers. At the end of each discussion, check with the child who raised the issue whether they feel this has helped. If it hasn't, further discussion may be required at a future group session or individual help may be needed from you or another competent person. Again, how to deal with such a situation is something that you could cover when setting ground rules.

Variation

To avoid children feeling exposed during the activity, you can have a school/class/group 'help box', where children can post their requests for help anonymously at any time. These can then be picked out at random at predetermined times for the whole group to offer possible answers/solutions to each issue drawn out of the box. A similar activity is the 'Problem-solving wall' (4.1.7), though that activity is specific to difficulties related to school work.

2.1.6 Activities from other chapters

The following activities from other chapters also help develop kindness and prosocial behaviour:

» 'Dance moves' (3.1.2)

» 'Decorate together' (3.2.2)

» 'Loving kindness meditation' (7.1.5)

» 'Helping my team' (9.1.1)

2.2 KINDNESS TO SELF

Kindness is not just something we extend to other people. Teaching children to be kind to themselves is also important, and something that some children may initially find challenging.

2.2.1 Advice letter

• **Recommended age**

8+

• **Duration**

15 minutes

- **Resources**

  » Scenario written on handouts or on the board

  » Paper

  » Pens

- **Method**

  Tell children that they will now read a scenario. They need to imagine this has happened to them, then write themselves a letter of advice on what to do; but to write the letter, they need to imagine what they would say to their best friend if this had happened to them instead:

  > *On Monday, your class had a test. You knew in advance there was going to be a test, and you did revise a little bit, but you had a sports competition at the weekend (you won), as well as a friend's birthday party, so you didn't spend as much time revising as you needed to. You didn't feel very confident about your test and struggled to answer some of the questions. You have been worried since you took the test and now, you get your result and haven't done as well as you would have liked to. You're upset and disappointed.*

■ 2.2.2 I matter

- **Recommended age**

  8+

- **Duration**

  15 minutes

- **Resources**

  » Paper

  » Pens

- **Method**

Read out the following instructions to pupils, then give them time to write the letter.

1. *Think of a problem you have or have had in the past, or something that is upsetting you now or has upset you in the past.*

2. *Give yourself advice on how to deal with it. Write it down, like a letter. Be kind to yourself and say the things you would say to your best friend if they had that problem.*

2.2.3 Self-kindness bingo

- **Recommended age**

  8+

- **Duration**

  30 minutes

- **Resources**

  » Paper (either plain paper, or with a pre-drawn grid containing 30 boxes)

  » Pens

- **Method**

Tell children they will now prepare an activity to help them be kind to themselves for up to 30 days. Explain that they will need to think of lots of things they can do that are good for them – things that make them feel good, relaxed and happy. First, they will need to come up with 30 self-kindness activities. You can start them off with examples and a short whole-class brainstorm, then split them into groups to continue the task. Examples could be 'colour in a picture' (see the 'Mindful colouring' activity, 7.2.2), 'breathing meditation' (see the 'Mindful breathing' activity, 7.1.2), 'listen to some music', 'read a book', etc.

Ask children to write their name and the title 'Kindness bingo' at the top of their sheet of paper.

As children discuss possible activities, they write one in each box of their grid until they have filled 30 boxes.

Over the next 30 days, they need to do as many of those activities as possible. They don't need to limit themselves to one per day! They can complete the activity early, and if they do, they may wish to create another bingo sheet to keep going.

Every few days, check in with them in lessons; find out how many activities they've done, and ask them to talk about how it felt to be kind to themselves.

2.2.4 Activities from other chapters

The following activities from other chapters also help develop self-kindness:

» 'Feel-good planner' (6.1.3)

» 'Best possible self' (6.1.4)

» Any activity from Chapter 7

2.3 WHOLE SCHOOL ACTIVITIES

There are many things you can do to make kindness part of your school's culture, from major projects and events to simple behaviour nudges (Halpern 2016).

2.3.1 T.H.I.N.K. before you speak

This mnemonic is one we have seen on posters in a few schools. Displaying such posters is an easy way of reminding pupils, staff and visitors to the school to follow its simple advice. Before you say something to someone, ask yourself whether it is:

» true

» helpful

» inspiring

» necessary

» kind.

This simple nudge (Halpern 2016) can prevent unnecessary arguments, as quite often we are all guilty of saying things we later regret when we realise we have hurt someone with our words.

▌ 2.3.2 Reverse advent calendar

This is something wonderful we have seen circulating on social media for individuals/families to do, but it would be a powerful kindness intervention with minimal cost to the participants if it was done by a whole school.

The idea is to discuss with a local charity (e.g. a food bank or homeless shelter) what donation items they would find useful, and potentially whether they could come and collect a lot of boxes containing donations from your school. You then aim to fill boxes with 25 items each over the month of December. Because schools won't be open for some of those days leading up to Christmas, you may wish to start your advent calendar in November.

Enlist the help of parents by telling them what you are doing, which charity the items will go to, and giving them a list of suggested items, in line with what the charity told you they need. Ask each parent to send one item in with their child. Teachers can co-ordinate this with their classes and year groups by allocating a day in the advent calendar to each child. It doesn't matter if there are more than 25 children in a class, as numbers can occur more than once. As a whole school, you will then simply fill however many 25-item boxes you end up with, and give any remaining items that don't make up a 25-item box to the charity as additional donations. Imagine how many people in need you can support by doing this! Even a small school with just 200 children could fill eight reverse advent calendars! And of course, staff would also participate, making the numbers even greater.

2.3.3 Activities from other chapters

» 'Let's help together' (3.3.1)

» 'Peer support' (9.3.3)

* Chapter 3 *

TEAMWORK

Teamwork is integral to belonging to the wider class, year group, and school community. When we think of teamwork, we often think of collaboration, support, bonding, aspects of positive relationships, trust building, and prosocial behaviours that are important for good mental health and happy schools (see also Chapter 9, 'Positive Relationships'). Collaboration is most intimately connected to the concept of teamwork, and collaborative teamwork benefits in school include higher academic achievement, improvement in attendance, increased motivation, and better relationships and communication skills (Nariman and Chrispeels 2016).

When we build effective teams in our schools, team performance improves, and through improvement, school innovation and performance increases (Somach and Drach-Zahavy 2007). Teams that use co-operative learning and interaction are particularly effective in schools; co-operative interaction is most effective at building positive peer relationships, and co-operative learning is using these positive peer relationships to maximise individual and group learning (Smith 1996). There are many types of co-operative learning structures, including formal, informal, short term, and long term; which structure you use depends on the activity or lesson that you are undertaking (see also the 'Co-operative learning' activity, 9.1.6). When using co-operative learning, you must ensure that teamwork skills are an essential part of the structure, and include opportunities for pupils to experience leadership, to make crucial decisions, effectively communicate their needs, and also learn how to manage conflict (Smith 1996). Co-operative learning and team building lend themselves well to cross-curricular applications and to a whole school approach.

When we speak of *team*, we really want you to think about the *who*, *how* and *why*. In a school community, the three main team players are the pupils, teachers and parents. If all three don't work together, you will have an inefficient team. This chapter will look at how you can build your teams and their team roles to help your pupils flourish, not only in school, but in all aspects of their lives.

Teamwork and character education

There are many ways to develop teamwork in your class, with more recent research focusing on using character traits and strengths that build teams and help them be more successful. The VIA Character Strengths[1] see teamwork as a 'blended strength' of character traits, including 'kindness, persistence, humility, and gratitude' (Peterson and Seligman 2004, p.360). In terms of character and larger institutions such as schools, teamwork is related to good citizenship, as well as the development of learning to play together and work together for the greater good. It is common in early childhood and pre-adolescent education that children will take part in activities such as team sports, choirs and plays (Peterson and Seligman 2004). You can use these activities to help build team skills that will have an impact across the curriculum subjects and into the wider school experience.

Teamwork is seen as a fulfilling aspect of being human and engaging with the wider community; it gives people a sense of belonging to something bigger than they are, and therefore increases their desire to do the right thing for the greater good. This makes teamwork a morally appropriate skill and character strength to develop, especially in young children, encouraging them to participate actively and openly in their class, school and community activities (Peterson and Seligman 2004).

---

1   www.viacharacter.org

Teamwork is labelled as a performance character trait by the Jubilee Centre for Character and Virtues,[2] but as teamwork is also linked to morally civic activities such as volunteering, community and citizenship, it can be taught within moral guidelines and a prosocial approach. In fact, the Jubilee Centre has conducted research into social action that indicates that thinking of, working with, and doing for others is a positive experience that can help build the character traits of young people and transform lives (Arthur, Harrison and Taylor 2015).

Building teams and teamwork skills also provides you with an active and engaging way to explore character education and character strengths, helping to bring character solidly into your school culture. By utilising teamwork as a character strength, you will teach children how to actively listen to others, respect other people's opinions, and spot and appreciate the character traits and strengths of others in their class and school (Niemiec 2018). These are skills that are required for flourishing, not only in school, but also in the workplace and wider community.

Will it always work?

Teamwork can be a great way to bond your class together and build better interpersonal relationships but it has its challenges. These include the possibility of unclear goals. When creating class goals, ensure that all pupils understand and value the goal. Focusing on teamwork can also limit the potential to develop leadership skills for some pupils. You may have shy pupils who will use teamwork activities and skills to blend into the crowd rather than attempting to be a leader. Ensure that when developing teamwork, you actively work with pupils who may struggle to step up to a leadership role.

On the other hand, some children, particularly younger ones, may find it difficult to focus on the greater good of the team, and be more inclined to focus on themselves. Becoming less self-centred and more in tune with the needs of others is part of childhood

---

2   www.jubileecentre.ac.uk

development, and by encouraging teamwork in your class, you can help children develop this skill. For those who struggle with working as a team, you may wish to introduce simple relationship building (see Chapter 9, 'Positive Relationships') and altruistic activities (see Chapter 2, 'Kindness') first.

3.1 COLLABORATIVE AND CO-OPERATIVE EFFORT

This set of activities will enhance your pupils' abilities to work together creatively and effectively, practise communication skills, and build positive relationships. Some of these activities can be done in larger groups or in pairs, and can easily cross from the classroom to the staffroom, so you can, if you wish, introduce any of these activities to your fellow teachers, to build staff morale and bonding.

3.1.1 Let's make it rain

This activity is a beautifully collaborative action that takes concentration, creativity, and working together to create 'rain' in the classroom. It can be a little noisy, so just be aware of other classrooms close by and make sure that you won't be disturbing any exams or tests (or even mindfulness activities) that are going on.

- **Recommended age**

  6+

- **Duration**

  5–10 minutes

- **Resources**

  » None

• Method

This activity can be done in the classroom and is a great way to energise your pupils and get them ready to work together at the beginning of the day. Once you have your class settled in their seats, divide them into four teams; to make it easier to instruct pupils and keep track of where you are up to in the activity. Name each team A, B, C and D, respectively and ensure pupils know which team they are in. Explain to them that you are going to make it rain and that each team has to pay attention to you as you will instruct them when to do each part of the activity. Before you begin the activity with them, show pupils the actions:

1. *Rub your palms together to make the sound of 'drizzle'.*

2. *Clap your hands together to make the sound of 'rain'.*

3. *Slap your thighs to make the sound of 'heavy rain'.*

4. *Stomp your feet to make the sound of 'hail'.*

Start with team A. Instruct them to do the first action (rub palms together). After a few moments, instruct team B to join in, then after a few moments instruct team C to join in, and finally, after a few moments instruct team D to join in.

Once everyone is rubbing their palms together, tell them to keep going, but then instruct team A to start clapping (while teams B, C and D continue rubbing their palms together), and slowly progress through the teams again until they are all clapping. Repeat this with the rest of the actions until all of your pupils are stomping their feet.

At this point let them make 'hail' for a few moments before you start to reverse the process: ask team D to stop stomping their feet and start slapping their thighs, and then team C, team B, and then team A. Then instruct team D to stop slapping their thighs and start clapping their hands instead, and repeat this with team C, B and A. Then, starting with team D again, ask them to stop clapping their hands and start rubbing their palms together instead, and ripple this through the teams from C to A, respectively. Finally, ask team

D to stop any noise-making action, then team C, team B and, as the room is almost quiet, get team A to stop and bring the class to complete quiet. Congratulate your pupils on how well they worked together and supported each other to make it rain.

3.1.2 Dance moves

Dancing (or the rhythmic behaviour shared by individuals) has been shown to increase co-operation, intentionality and prosocial behaviours, so dancing and music is a great way to bring pupils together to bond as a team (Reddish, Fischer and Bulbulia 2013). In this activity you will be using co-operation and synchronicity to build a sense of team in your pupils.

- **Recommended age**

  5+

- **Duration**

  10 minutes

- **Resources**

  » Music and the means to play it through a loudspeaker in class

- **Method**

  Once you have a couple of appropriate songs ready to play, arrange your class in a circle. Explain to pupils what they will do and have a volunteer ready to start the activity. Start the music. Your starter pupil will begin the activity by demonstrating a dance move, then either going clockwise or anticlockwise around the circle, each student will copy the dance move. Once the first dance move has made it around the circle to the pupil who started it, the pupil next to them demonstrates a new dance move. The other pupils will keep on doing the original dance move until the new one reaches them as it goes around the circle. Keep the activity going around the circle until every child has had a chance to contribute a dance move.

If a pupil struggles to come up with a dance move, tell them that they can repeat a dance move that has already gone around the circle. If you want to stop the activity after one loop of the circle has been completed, that is fine, but if you have the time and inclination, keep the dance moves going around for as long as you like.

3.1.3 Last letter, first letter

This is an activity that actively engages your pupils' self-control and communication skills. A variation on an old classic and inspired by the ImprovHQ[3] team's interpretation, this activity involves each child taking a turn to say a sentence to their partner. Their partner then responds by starting the first word in their sentence with the last letter of the first person's last word. This may take a while for the children to get to grips with, but that is part of the fun! It will teach them that it's OK to make mistakes, and helping them develop their listening skills will increase their ability to engage with others and collaborate.

If pupils struggle to think of a first sentence, you can start off the activity by giving them all the same sentence to start with. As a variation, you can also do this activity in a circle rather than in pairs.

- **Recommended age**

  10+

- **Duration**

  5–10 minutes

- **Resources**

  » None

---

3 www.improvhq.com

- **Method**

  Divide the children into pairs (or small groups) and explain the rules of the activity to them. You may wish to do a demonstration by having the conversation with one of the pupils. For example:

  > YOU: Today I am going to the park in the afternoon with my sister. (I have ended the last word with the letter 'r', so the first word in your answer needs to start with the letter 'r'.)

  > PUPIL: Really, that sounds like a lot of fun. What are you going to do?

  > YOU: Offer to push her on the swing!

  > PUPIL: Great! I wish my sister would do that for me.

  After the demonstration, ensure pupils have understood what they need to do and get them to start the activity. Have a time limit to the activity, and after each pair have had a go, swap pupils so that they learn to engage, co-operate and communicate carefully with a wide range of people.

3.2 CHARACTER STRENGTHS AND TEAMWORK

Much research has been undertaken into character strengths and the impact these can have on wellbeing and success (for more information, see the introduction to Section 1, 'Character Education'). Teamwork is a character strength associated with citizenship (community), the building of 'social trust' (Niemiec 2018, p.11) and the development of positive views of others (Niemiec 2018). Using character strengths from a team perspective means that pupils become stronger at recognising other people's character strengths, and character terminology will become part of their everyday language. They will see that when people use their diverse strengths as part of a team, this fosters a sense of social belonging and trust.

3.2.1 Character strengths class tree

This activity is inspired by the 'Family Strengths Tree' activity created by Rashid (2015). It helps pupils understand the character strengths of one of their key teams – their class. It can also help them to clearly see the dynamics and relationships between their classmates and how they can use their strengths with others to build positive relationships and stronger teams. You will need to access the VIA Character Strengths[4] for this activity.

- **Recommended age**

  8+

- **Duration**

  20–30 minutes

- **Resources**

  » Pens, pencils or paint

  » Paper and/or card

- **Method**

  A class tree is like a family tree. Ask your pupils to each, individually, create a class tree, writing down each member of their class (including teacher and any classroom assistants), and drawing lines to create connections (such as friendships, relations, sporting teams, those with similar interests or hobbies, etc.). For each person in the class tree, ask your pupils to write down two to three character strengths that they have observed. Once the children have completed the class tree of strengths, open up a discussion in class about who shows which strengths, and how. As each child will have created their tree individually, each pupil should have a wide variety of strengths attributed to them, as observed by their classmates.

---

4   www.viacharacter.org

▪ 3.2.2 Decorate together

In addition to teamwork, this activity will allow your pupils to explore character strengths such as creativity, appreciation of beauty and excellence, zest and kindness. It could be an activity you do in the classroom (or you could do a classroom swap with another class), or you could take it out into the school or even the wider community (with relevant permissions, as it will involve decorating a particular area, such as a wall, fence, door, patch of grass, etc.). Just be aware that this activity may take a little extra organising on your part, so it may be best suited to do once a term or even just once a year.

- **Recommended age**

  6+

- **Duration**

  1–3 hours (depending on the location)

- **Resources**

  » Decorative supplies, such as paper, streamers, pictures, pens, paint, etc.

  » Smocks or shirts for the pupils to protect their clothing

- **Method**

  Decide where you are going to decorate: perhaps a corner or a wall in your classroom, a hallway or a door in your school, or you may even be able to get permission to decorate a wall in a nursing home or a garden wall at a hospital. For this method's explanation we will use a wall in your classroom as an example, but don't be afraid to think big.

  Explain to your pupils that you are going to use your character strengths to decorate this wall in your classroom, that everyone will get a turn to contribute, and that you are going to support and help each other to make it an inspiring and beautiful wall. Show your pupils the supplies, and spend some time discussing how best to decorate the area – invite input from all pupils and reach agreement by consensus or vote before starting the practical decorating task.

Then ask pupils to put their protective smocks or shirts on, and start decorating. If you have a large class, perhaps it would be better to divide the pupils into smaller teams and give each team responsibility for different aspects of decorating the wall. For example, one team could be in charge of hanging streamers, another team in charge of painting the wall, and perhaps another team in charge of tidying up at the end! Everyone has their role to play and this is important to emphasise. If you split the class into teams in this way, you will need to have other activities for children to work on while they are not actively engaged in the decorating activity.

Once you have finished decorating, clean up, pack away the supplies, and encourage your class to sit back and admire their handiwork and team effort.

3.3 WHOLE SCHOOL ACTIVITIES

A whole school approach to teamwork is important, and should include pupils, all staff, and parents. You may occasionally need to split the school into smaller teams and let the effects ripple out. For greater impact, you could form cross-departmental teams. Try to engage parents if you can. Parental involvement, especially in the earlier school years, is crucial. It promotes positive experiences of school for the pupils and also positively impacts on the self-development and parenting skills of the parents (Hill and Taylor 2004).

3.3.1 Let's help together

Find a local community-based project that the school as a whole can support. Perhaps hold a school-wide fundraiser to raise money for an important local cause, or hold a fun-run that will raise awareness of a local issue. Ensure that parents and staff are as involved as the pupils.

3.3.2 Family–pupil–teacher bond

Hold a special afternoon or evening where families and pupils can come to school and learn more about the benefits of teamwork for themselves and the school. Provide a little bit of context and information about teamwork and how it can help the children, then run a few teamwork activities. Here are some activity suggestions:

My family's favourite
Around the hall or classroom lay out pictures of different foods or cuisines. Ask families to go and stand next to their favourite food. This should create groups formed of teachers, pupils and their families. In these family–pupil–teacher groups, they now discuss how and why they enjoy the food.

Things we have in common
This is a great activity for teachers and parents to learn and acknowledge the similarities they share. Each teacher should pair up with a parent, and together discover five things they have in common. Once they discover five things they have in common, they repeat the process with another teacher/parent. If there are more parents than teachers, parents can pair up with other parents, but try to ensure that the teachers reach as many parents as possible.

'Thank you' notes
Write a 'Thank you' note (or notes) to a parent who has done something lovely for the school. Do this with no expectation of anything in return. This is gratitude in action that will impact on wider team morale and encourage parents to feel more welcome. For more gratitude and kindness ideas, take a look at Chapter 1, 'Gratitude', and Chapter 2, 'Kindness'.

* Chapter 4 *

LOVE OF LEARNING

A love of learning, not just of the education provided by the curriculum, but also a love of learning about life, meaning, and what really, truly interests them, is one of the greatest gifts you can give your pupils. In terms of character, and in particular the VIA Character Strengths,[1] love of learning is a key strength that helps us acquire and use new information. It can be developed and strengthened with targeted activities.

In the VIA Character Strengths categorisation, love of learning comes under the virtue of *wisdom* and the intellectual/cognitive strengths. The benefits of developing a love of learning, noted by Peterson and Seligman (2004), include being more adept at seeking and handling challenges, becoming more resourceful, seeing more possibilities, increased self-efficacy (for more information about self-efficacy see Chapter 10, 'Goal-Setting and Achievement'), and decreased levels of stress. Research shows that, in the UK, love of learning is one of the top five character strengths embodied by both men and women, with open-mindedness, fairness, curiosity and kindness being the other four (Linley *et al.* 2007).

Love of learning, like many character strengths, should not be developed in isolation, but rather within the context of the other strengths. Schwartz and Sharpe (2006) talk of certain strengths that should not be developed in isolation, their examples being love of learning and curiosity, determining that these two particular

---

1   www.viacharacter.org

strengths would not help a person in a 'mundane social situation' (p.386). They also advise being mindful that there are other character traits out there beyond the VIA Character Strengths, including the virtue of *phronesis*, also known as *practical wisdom*. Phronesis, as described by the Jubilee Centre for Character and Virtues (2017), is the virtue that will integrate and connect all other character traits and virtues; it is cultivated through experience and reflection, and helps us develop the ability to discern and react appropriately to day-to-day situations.

So, what constitutes a love of learning? According to Park and Peterson (2006b), it is the mastery of new skills, exploration of new topics and themes, stepping up to intellectual challenges, and recognising the boundless possibilities to learn every day. Wagner and Ruch (2015) also strongly demonstrate that cultivating love of learning increases academic achievement.

Will it always work?

One thing to be aware of is the overuse and underuse of this character strength. Recent research has indicated that the positive effects of using character strengths are weakened if we overuse or underuse any strength. Overuse of love of learning could present itself in a child as a form of elitism or snobbery – a 'know-it-all' attitude – or fixation on a particular topic to the exclusion of others, whilst the underuse of love of learning in a child could present as complacency and a lack of caring towards learning new things and seeking challenges (Niemiec 2018). To avoid the overuse and underuse of any character strength it is important to teach your pupils about context – when and where it is appropriate to use that particular strength. Love of learning is an appropriate strength to use in the classroom, but even then you can be faced with the issues described above. If you face issues of overuse or underuse, you could have a conversation with the individual pupil, or even a class discussion, about when it is and isn't appropriate to use certain strengths. For example, you could ask and have group or class discussions about questions such as:

- *When you love learning so much that you don't get enough sleep at night because you want to know everything there is to know about a topic, is that healthy?*

- *If you really love learning and keep telling your friends about everything you know about a subject, when does it become 'bragging'? If it is making your friends feel bad because they don't know as much, is it a good thing? If not, how could you share your learning in a way that is helpful, instead?* [Here you could, for example, introduce the 'Co-operative learning' activity (9.1.6).]

Research also suggests that love of learning (along with creativity, appreciation of beauty, and modesty) do not necessarily correlate with increased life-satisfaction (Lounsbury *et al.* 2009; Park and Peterson 2006a). This does not mean that we should not work on these character strengths, but it solidifies the argument that strengths should not be treated as islands, to be developed on their own and without context. Remember that love of learning is just one tool of many that can help increase the life-satisfaction and wellbeing of your pupils.

4.1 CLASSROOM ACTIVITIES

The classroom is one of the easiest places to develop a love of learning in your pupils, and the added advantage is that you can really explore this strength in your curriculum. These activities are easily embedded across different subjects. Below are many avenues for developing a love of learning, and simultaneously learning about other character strengths, especially through story, research and discussion. Have fun with this chapter, be imaginative and playful, and role-model your own love of learning.

4.1.1 Discover something new

This activity will develop a sense of curiosity and the desire to observe and learn during an activity that the pupil may consider mundane and/or boring. This is based on a curiosity intervention by Niemiec (2018).

- **Recommended age**

  6+

- **Duration**

  Depends on the activity chosen by the pupil

- **Resources**

  » Pens

  » Paper

- **Method**

  Ask your pupils to select an activity – from school or home – that they find boring, and write it on a piece of paper. Explain to them that when they encounter that activity that day they have to really pay attention to what they are doing and discover two to three new things about the activity that they didn't know before. When they come into school the next day, ask them to write down the things that they observed and learnt. The level and complexity of writing will depend on the age and maturity of the child. An example could be:

  > *Washing dishes is boring. Today while I washed the dinner dishes, I noticed that the bubbles all had rainbow colours in them. I felt that the water didn't cool down quickly, and I realised that my sister was very quick at drying the dishes after I placed them in the drying rack.*

Get them either to continue doing this activity and writing down their observations for a week, or change the activity that they do each day.

4.1.2 Beautiful things

This activity is another variation of one of Niemiec's (2018) interventions. Along with love of learning, it promotes the strength of Appreciation of Beauty and Excellence. You can do this activity as a one-off or make it a regular practice in your class.

- **Recommended age**

  8+

- **Duration**

  5–10 minutes

- **Resources**

  » Pens

  » Paper (or journal/diary)

- **Method**

  Ask your pupils to write down these three instructions at the top of their page:

  1. *Observe and describe something new and unique you have noticed in nature.*

  2. *Observe and describe something new and unique you have observed that is man-made.*

  3. *Observe and describe something new and unique you have noticed in your friends/family.*

Explain that you are going to do this activity for 'x' amount of days/ weeks, and that each day, they will answer these questions. Ensure that your pupils write a few sentences for each heading and really describe in detail what they have observed.

4.1.3 I'll look into that

We all know children who will answer a question with 'I don't know' or 'I don't care'. This activity will help them, as well as your other pupils, to change their perspective and seek answers to questions they don't know the answer to.

- **Recommended age**

  8+

- **Duration**

  Depends on the question and the depth of research needed for the answer

- **Resources**

  » Pens

  » Paper (or journal/diary)

- **Method**

  Set up a rule in your classroom: if your pupils (or you – this is a great opportunity for role-modelling!) don't know the answer to a question, they have to respond by saying, 'I will look into that'. If a pupil says they will look into something, give them the time and space to do some research. Once they have discovered the answer, they can report it back to the class. In terms of reporting back to you and the class, they can either write a report, create index cards and give a talk in front of the class on the question/answer, or discuss it one-on-one with another pupil, who can then discuss it with another pupil, and so on (see also 'Co-operative learning', 9.1.6). Decide, with the pupil, on the best method of reporting back.

4.1.4 Classroom book club

Engage with other learners around you and start a classroom book club. This is another variation on the 'Co-operative learning' activity (9.1.6).

- **Recommended age**

  8+

- **Duration**

  The length of time needed to read a book in class (either independently for each pupil or read by the teacher to the class), plus 20–40 minutes for discussion time as a class and repeat with cross-class groups

- **Resources**

  » Books

  » Pens

  » Paper (or journal/diary)

- **Method**

  Join up with your neighbouring class(es) and each take turns to select a book that the classes will read for that month. Pupils can either read the book individually, or it can be a class reading activity where you read a few chapters from the book to your pupils every day (this will also depend on the age of the pupils). At the end of the month, first discuss with your class what they thought about the book and what they learnt from it. Next, bring the classes together and divide the children into cross-class groups to discuss the book together. When you are back in your own class, ask your pupils if they learnt anything new from the other class.

▨ 4.1.5 Character strengths at the movies

This activity is based on an intervention that explores the motivating powers of story and film (Niemiec 2018). You can use this activity alongside cross-curricular themes and explore the character strengths shown by historical, scientific and creative role-models. We have included this activity in this chapter, but it can be used to explore any character strengths. It is a particularly good activity to explore multiple character strengths together.

- **Recommended age**

  8+

- **Duration**

  1–3 hours (recommended as half-day activity, or you may choose to split it over several lessons)

- **Resources**

  » Full movie (or selected clips of movies that illustrate the character strengths you wish to explore with your pupils)

  » TV or screen in room, speakers, etc.

  » Pens

  » Paper

- **Method**

  Select a movie that is age- and theme-appropriate (we have made some suggestions below). If you do not have enough time to present the whole movie to the class, select clips of the movie that illustrate the strengths you wish to explore, or show the movie over a number of lessons. Explain to the pupils that, as they watch the movie, they should think about the actions and motives of the characters, and be aware of how watching the movie makes them feel.

Once you have finished watching the movie (or clips), ask your pupils to consider and write down responses to the following questions:

1. *How did the movie make you feel?* [See also the similar activity focusing on emotions, 'Inside out' (6.2.1).]

2. *What most inspired you about the movie?*

3. *Write down the character strengths that you noticed in a character and how they showed them.*

4. *Is there a way you can use one of the character strengths shown in the movie in your own life?*

An add-on to this activity would be to have an open discussion in class about what character strengths the pupils noticed in the movie and how these strengths can translate into their everyday lives.

Some suggested movies:

» *Frozen* (Del Vecho, Buck and Lee 2013)

» *The Wizard of Oz* (LeRoy and Flemming 1939)

» *Mary Poppins* (Walsh and Stevenson 1964)

» *Brave* (Sarafian, Andrews *et al.* 2012)

» *Charlotte's Web* (Kerner, Winley and Winick 2006)

» *Toy Story* (Arnold, Guggenheim and Lasseter 1995)

» *The Incredibles* (Walker and Bird 2004)

▧ 4.1.6 Word lottery

Expand your pupils' vocabulary and understanding of words by playing 'Word lottery'.

- **Recommended age**

  5+

- **Duration**

  20–30 minutes

- **Resources**

  » Dictionary/computer

  » Pens

  » Paper

- **Method**

  Place enough words for the number of pupils that you have, on scraps of paper, in a hat or box. Make sure that the words are ones they may not have heard of or not know very well. Walk around your class with the hat or box and ask pupils each to pull a word out. Explain to them that they will have all day or week to research and discover all that they can about that word – how to pronounce it, where it comes from, what it means, how to use it – and provide examples. To help with their research, they can use a dictionary, a computer, and/or ask friends, teachers, siblings, parents, etc. The depth of research they do and resources they access will depend on their age. By the end of the day or week all of the pupils will have to explain to the class – just in a sentence or two – what their word means and how to use it.

4.1.7 Problem-solving wall

This activity is relevant to a number of the topics covered in this book, including teamwork and goal-setting. It also encourages open discussion about academic problems that your pupils may have and helps them realise that they can learn from their peers and teach (or support) each other (see also 'Co-operative learning', 9.1.6).

- **Recommended age**

  8+

- **Duration**

  10–15 minutes

- **Resources**

  » Blank wall

  » Pens

  » Paper

  » Sticky tape or other appropriate adhesive

- **Method**

  Allocate a blank wall or part of wall to be your 'problem-solving wall'. Explain to your pupils that throughout the day, if they are really struggling with any of their class work, they can write their problem down and stick it on the wall. They can either sign their note or write it anonymously. At the end of the day, you can then choose one or two problems that your pupils may be struggling with and open the solution up to the whole class, by either leading a discussion about the problem, or pairing pupils up to further discuss and resolve the issue.

■ 4.1.8 Your challenge

This activity will allow for some autonomy in choosing and researching a particular theme or topic. It will help teach pupils how powerful knowledge is and that, with the ability to research and understand any topic, they could undertake almost any challenge. It also ties in with Chapter 10, 'Goal-Setting and Achievement', and could be used in conjunction with the 'Goal map' activity (10.1.1).

- **Recommended age**

  10+

- **Duration**

  10 minutes on the first day to explain the activity, plus 1 week or multiple weeks (you decide how long to allocate to research), plus 1 hour on the last day for pupils to present back to class

- **Resources**

  » Library/computer

  » Pens

  » Paper

- **Method**

  Ask your pupils to choose a particular challenge that they may be facing now or a potential future goal, then ask them to spend time researching this challenge and write a report on their findings.

  As part of the process, encourage them to look at what makes this challenge a challenge and how they can overcome it (or achieve their goal). Include key details such as steps that need to be taken, safety issues, etc. Also prompt them to research others (role-models) who have overcome or achieved a similar problem, and consider how these people have tackled the challenge. Inspire your pupils to go as in-depth as they possibly can.

They can either prepare their findings as a report to hand in to you and have a subsequent discussion with you about, or do a short presentation to the whole class explaining what they have learnt about the challenge they are facing or goal they want to achieve. Some examples of challenges include: bungee jumping, raising huge amounts of money for a charity, swimming at the national championships, volunteering for a whole year in a nursing home, getting into a top university, scuba diving to a shipwreck. The possibilities are endless; encourage your pupils to think big!

4.2 WHOLE SCHOOL ACTIVITIES

School is – or should be, in our view – in great part about pupils developing a love of learning, so it seems only natural that a whole school approach to a love of learning should and could happen. These activities will help you embed a love of learning across the school, not just for pupils, but also for staff and the wider community.

4.2.1 School-wide book club

This is variation on the 'Classroom book club' activity (4.1.4). Follow the same instructions but simply extend it out to the whole school. Group certain classes together – perhaps across age groups as well, as this could make for a chance to really see different perspectives on the book – for discussion of the book at the end of the month.

4.2.2 Art gallery

Ask each year group to choose a theme, and encourage all pupils and staff to create an artwork based on that theme. It can be anything that can be seen as 'art': a drawing, painting, sculpture, poem, story, or piece of music, for example. Then set up a school-wide 'art gallery', showcasing the artwork (which may include performances of art such as music or poetry). Each year group can display their artwork in specific areas of the school that are accessible and easy for parents to come and visit if they wish; or invite parents to a special performance and display evening. Encourage pupils and staff to go and visit each area and see the art, or to attend the performances of other year groups.

4.2.3 What I learnt this week/month

A pupil or member of staff volunteer each week or month to do a short presentation, during assembly, about something interesting they have recently learnt – the more obscure and unusual, the better. The presentation should be lively and interesting and can include any support materials the individual would like (e.g. music, pictures, objects). Allow time at the end of the presentation for the audience to ask two to three questions about the topic.

∗ Chapter 5 ∗

SELF-REFLECTION

Self-reflection is one of the key aspects of developing and building character in our pupils. Teaching self-reflection techniques to pupils will help them *grow into their character*, understand at a deeper level their *core values*, develop the ability to live by these core values, and contribute positively to the world around them (Lickona, Schaps and Lewis 2002). The Jubilee Centre for Character and Virtues (2016) describes self-reflection as being about the *how* and *why* of what you have done, as well as examining the thoughts and feelings that surround an event, and how that may have impacted on you.

As a skill, self-reflection takes time to develop (Harrison, Morris and Ryan 2016). It underpins all of the character traits and wellbeing activities mentioned in this book, and beyond. Regarded as a key element of many educational theories, self-reflection is an important part of the learning process, whether for life skills or academic learning. Kolb (1984) developed the model for experiential learning, which comprises four elements: *concrete experience*; *observation and reflection*; *formation of abstract concepts*; *testing concepts in new situations*. What the model cycle suggests is that experience leads to observation and reflection, which then leads to new ideas and concepts, which may change future actions (Roberts 2008). This perpetual spiral upwards in terms of self-knowledge and growth means that the pupil can develop critical thinking skills, not just related to academic work but also in other aspects of their lives. Self-discovery is inevitable when engaging with self-reflection; assumptions can be questioned, and opinions changed (Mezirow 1998; Roberts 2008).

Roberts (2008) believes that the *action–reflection cycle* should begin from early in the pupil's educational experience, meaning that self-reflection should be taught from a young age. As a concept, though, self-reflection may be new to your pupils and it is something that you may have to spend some time on, explaining and role-modelling. Try to make the self-reflection process a natural part of the curriculum, as suggested by the Jubilee Centre for Character and Virtues (2016). This may challenge current structures of education in your school, but it is worth the effort to enable your pupils to start to engage with life from a critical perspective. Develop a variety of ways to encourage self-reflection in the school, ensuring that pupils understand what is expected of them.

Self-reflection can also build the moral and ethical values of pupils; as your self-reflective skill increases, you can bring the technique into interpersonal relationships, drawing upon previous experiences and feelings to understand and relate to others (Grey 2004). We explore interpersonal relationships further in Chapter 9, 'Positive Relationships'. The Jubilee Centre for Character and Virtues (2016) also explores the moral and ethical considerations of self-reflection, stating that the development of virtues and character is dependent on the ability to self-reflect. To react to any given situation with appropriate responses, emotions and actions shows the ability to reflect in that moment on what is morally right (Wright, Morris and Bawden 2014).

Don't limit the practice of self-reflection to just the pupils; role-model the practice. Ensure that you talk about your self-reflection practice with pupils and let them know the processes and discoveries that you have made about yourself. When using self-reflection, it is important to approach the practice with an open mind, wholeheartedly engage with the process, and work with it responsibly (Dewey 1933). Approaching self-reflection with these attitudes will give the process real depth, as well as 'infuse the activity with meaning and vitality' (Dinkelman 2003, p.9).

Will it always work?

When children are first introduced to self-reflection, they may resist the process and expect to be provided with answers, not just to academic problems but to everyday life situations, too. If that is the case, you can gently coach a child along the process, by asking them to talk you through a situation, asking questions such as: *What happened? What happened next? Why do you think X responded that way? Would you do anything differently if you could? How else could you have said that? Why do you think you reacted that way?* and so on.

Self-reflection, however, is not the only – and not always the best – way to learn and progress in any given activity. If a pupil doesn't understand a maths problem, no amount of self-reflection is going to help them discover the answer. Ensure that self-reflection is considered as part of a toolkit of learning, both academically and personally. Other tools should include: dialogue and discussion with peers, teachers and family members; and enquiry and research (Bengtsson 1995).

It is also important to be aware that, while research shows that self-reflection can have a positive impact on mental health issues such as depression, if it turns into self-rumination, the positive benefits can be negated (Takano and Tanno 2009). To ensure that self-reflection doesn't become self-rumination, ensure that your pupils are growing and learning from the process and not getting stuck in negative thought patterns. Make sure that they understand what self-reflection is and how it can help them, and if you have any concerns about any negative thoughts or patterns that become apparent, address them privately with the pupil and ensure that they get the correct help that they need.

▦ 5.1 CLASSROOM ACTIVITIES ▦▦▦▦▦▦▦▦

Self-reflection is an activity that can easily slip into different subjects in your class. It can be a nice start or ending to the day, and become a part of your pupils' daily school habits. You can theme your self-reflections by day or month, perhaps using some of the activities from other chapters of the book to kick-start some self-reflection ideas. Chapter 1, 'Gratitude', is a great place to start with this. Be creative, make the process positive and productive and, most importantly, role-model self-reflection yourself.

▦ 5.1.1 Self-reflection learning journal

This activity is a general start to self-reflection (though once pupils start to get the hang of self-reflection journalling you could start to bring in specific themes and questions for them to journal about). This journal is private for the pupils. Let them know that no one else can look in it without their permission. Do make sure that if any pupils are struggling with journalling, or if journalling raises any problems or concerns, they feel they can come and talk to you privately about these issues.

- **Recommended age**

    8+

- **Duration**

    5–10 minutes per day

- **Resources**

    » Pens

    » Paper (perhaps in journal form so that they can keep the journal throughout the school year)

Method

Decide on starter questions that you can use to kick-start your pupils' self-reflection learning journals each week (see below for some examples). Starter questions allow you to help focus the pupils' self-enquiry so they can progress from week to week. You can have a weekly or daily self-reflection journalling session, and can set a new starter question each day, week or month. On the first day, explain to them what the self-reflection journals are for – below is some suggested wording:

> Today we are going to start keeping a self-reflection journal. Self-reflection is when you think about the actions, emotions and thoughts that you have had today and you think about what went well, what could have gone better and how you can improve next time. Each week, I will give you a question that you will reflect on every day. I will ask you to write for five minutes each day about this question, and your actions, emotions and thoughts that link to that question. I want you to be as honest as possible; nobody else will see your journal unless you give them permission.

If some pupils are still unclear about what self-reflection is or how to journal, you can take some one-on-one time with them to discuss further what is expected.

Some suggested journalling starter questions:

» *What went well? Why?*

» *What success did you have today? Why was it a success?*

» *What was challenging today? Why was it challenging? How could you improve?*

» *How did you behave today? What affected your behaviour?*

» *What character strength(s) did you use today? How did you use it/them? How did you feel when you used it/them?*

◼ 5.1.2 Build up your character strengths

This activity will make use of the VIA Character Strengths,[1] so to make it easier for pupils to choose a strength they want to build on, list them at the start of this activity. Research (Seligman *et al.* 2005) has shown that using one of our *signature strengths* – top five strengths – in a new way each day for seven days can reduce the symptoms of depression and increase happiness for six months. You can, however, also use this activity to help pupils develop one of their less prominent strengths further.

- **Recommended age**

  9+

- **Duration**

  10–20 minutes

- **Resources**

  » Pens

  » Paper

- **Method**

  Explain to your pupils that you are going to look at character strengths that they may not feel are as prominent for them as other strengths. (Alternatively, explain to them that they are going to pick one of their strongest strengths and find new ways of using it. If you choose this option, it may help to do the 'Strengths-Based Activities', 9.2, first.) Ask them to pick a strength that they want to work on and write this down. Then ask them to write down how they could use this strength differently or more often on a day-to-day basis.

---

1   www.viacharacter.org

5.1.3 Story time

This activity asks your students to publicly reflect on using their character strengths. You will need to list the VIA Character Strengths[2] for them to refer to.

- **Recommended age**

  5+

- **Duration**

  10–20 minutes

- **Resources**

  » None

- **Method**

  Ask your pupils to think of a recent moment when they were doing their best or where they had a success. Select a few pupils to stand up and tell the class their story. Once the pupil has told their story, ask the rest of the pupils to identify and tell the story-telling pupil what character strengths they displayed in their story. This activity is a variation on Step 2 in the 'Using strengths cards' activity (9.2.3).

5.1.4 Thinking about my behaviour

Use this activity on an individual basis. If you have a pupil who is particularly struggling with behaviour in some way, this activity can give them a chance to self-reflect on their behaviour and how it may impact on others.

- **Recommended age**

  6+

---

2   www.viacharacter.org

- **Duration**

  5 minutes

- **Resources**

  » Pens

  » Paper

- **Method**

  If you have a pupil exhibiting challenging behaviour, have a discreet private conversation with them outside of or after class, and ask them to answer these questions (either ask them to write the answers down or to answer them in discussion with you):

  1. *What behaviour today has led to you having this conversation with me today?*

  2. *Why did you behave that way?*

  3. *How can we work together to ensure that this behaviour doesn't happen again?*

  If they are answering these questions in discussion with you, let them lead the discussion, allowing them plenty of time to reflect and answer the questions, and really engage in listening to their answers.

5.1.5 My mood

This activity will help your pupils track and understand how and why their moods change throughout the day. You may find it helpful to do one or more of the 'Emotional Granularity' activities (6.2) before doing this activity.

- **Recommended age**

  5+

- **Duration**

  20 minutes on the first day (to set up the grid and explain the activity), plus 5 minutes on subsequent days

- **Resources**

  » Pens

  » Paper

- **Method**

  On the first day, explain to your pupils that they are going to track their moods. Ask them to draw a grid on a piece of paper or in a school workbook/diary. Across the top of the grid, they need to label each column with the days of the week (Monday, Tuesday, Wednesday, etc.).

  Down the left-hand side, they need to label each row with different times of the day, making each row deep enough to allow space for writing (you may wish to provide younger pupils with a grid already drawn up):

  » *Morning*

  » *Lunchtime*

  » *Afternoon*

  » *Night time*

  Once the pupils have created their grid, tell them that when they come to school in the morning the first thing they are going to do is draw an 'emoticon' that reflects their mood – it might be a smiley face, a sad face, an angry face, a bored face, etc. (show them examples if you need to) – in the morning row for that day. Next to their 'emoticon' they write, briefly, why they feel that way. Repeat for the lunchtime and afternoon row. They will need to complete the night time row at home.

▨ 5.2 WHOLE SCHOOL ACTIVITIES ▨▨▨▨▨▨

Whole school self-reflection is a great way to get teachers and the leadership team involved in role-modelling self-reflection.

▨ 5.2.1 Whole school evaluation

This isn't one activity, but rather a signposting to the Jubilee Centre for Character and Virtues (2016) *Character Education Evaluation Handbook for Schools.* This handbook provides you with some theoretical and conceptual background to self-reflection and evaluation for schools.

▨ 5.2.2 Class moods

This is an extension of the individual 'My mood' activity (5.1.5). Each class draws up a grid, but they log the general class mood at the end of each day. To do this, you can take a tally at the end of each day of how pupils are feeling. To encourage pupils to be as honest as possible, you can do it anonymously by having them draw on a scrap of paper the 'emoticon' that corresponds to how they feel. Each week, the class teacher can go to a larger grid that is on display in school (in the office, the hall, etc.) and log what their class's moods have been that week. This is a great way to track the whole school's moods and to get an idea of when during the week pupils are happiest, grumpiest, excited, etc. This is also a variation on the 'Emotional temperature' activity (6.3.3).

▨ 5.2.3 Activities from other chapters

» 'Emotions assembly' (6.3.1)

» 'Mindfulness dots' (7.3.4). You can add an extra element to this activity for the whole school by asking pupils and staff to spend a moment thinking about how they are feeling and why.

POSITIVE
EDUCATION

According to Seligman *et al.* (2009), schools focus too much on academic success factors and discipline, and not enough on the wellbeing and happiness of children, against a backdrop of rising rates of depression amongst the young. They also make the case for schools being an ideal environment for initiatives to improve children's and adolescents' wellbeing, as that is where they spend most of their time. They argue that such initiatives can measurably improve young people's wellbeing, as well as their behaviour, and that they can improve pupils' educational engagement and academic success.

Shoshani and Steinmetz (2014) also highlight the global tendency towards increasingly challenging academic rigour in schools, and the worrying rise of depression and other mental health disorders in adolescents. They point to a number of studies showing that positive psychology interventions play an important role in improving children's and adolescents' happiness and wellbeing. Norrish *et al.* (2013) also point to concerns regarding the mental health of adolescents and young adults, and to the value of schools as a setting for the implementation of positive psychology interventions for the improvement of young people's wellbeing. They describe positive education as 'bringing together the science of Positive Psychology with best-practice teaching to encourage and support schools and individuals within their communities to flourish' (p.148) and define flourishing as including elements of both eudaimonic and hedonistic happiness (see explanation in the introduction to Chapter 6, 'Happiness and Positive Emotions'). They highlight research that further supports the notion that flourishing enhances academic achievement.

This section of the book will help you bring positive education into your classroom, as well as embed it into the culture of your school, to enhance the wellbeing of your pupils and the entire school community, as well as to positively impact on your pupils' academic success as they progress through their educational journey.

Chapter 6

HAPPINESS AND POSITIVE EMOTIONS

Questions about what *happiness* is, and how it can be achieved, have been discussed for centuries. The concept of *eudaimonia* (Oxford Reference 2005) dates back to Aristotle and is often used to describe happiness but also includes concepts of virtue and goodness. *Eudaimonic happiness* is often contrasted with *hedonic happiness* (Blackburn 2016), which is generally seen as the pursuit of pleasure. Psychologists have been debating whether these are two separate experiences of happiness or simply different ways of looking at the same thing. Biswas-Diener, Kashdan and King (2009) maintain that it is the latter, and that studying happiness from a variety of perspectives is 'instructive and important' (p.210).

Cohn *et al.* (2009) offer a broader description of happiness, as 'a composite of life satisfaction, coping resources, and positive emotions' (p.361), and Delle Fave *et al.*'s (2011) analysis of data from hundreds of research participants spanning three continents found happiness to include 'an even and peaceful attitude in dealing with life events, be they pleasant or unpleasant, and in achieving a balance between different needs, commitments and aspirations' (p.204). They explain that this element is derived from traditions in both Western and Asian cultures.

Happiness is therefore a complex term that encompasses many elements, including morality and values, pleasure/hedonism/

positive emotions, and an attitude that allows us to find peace in both joyful and difficult times.

Emotions underpin most of human behaviour. How we feel impacts on how we interact with other people, how easily we can concentrate on our work, and how well we overcome obstacles/ bounce back from setbacks (*resilience*). *Positive emotions* are intricately linked with happiness, which is why we are covering both topics together in this chapter.

Positive emotions, which are mostly fleeting, have been found to be better at predicting growth of internal resources, such as resilience, than *general life satisfaction*, which is also often used interchangeably with happiness (Cohn *et al.* 2009). This is linked to the 'upward spirals' (Fredrickson 2001, p.223) in wellbeing that, according to Fredrickson's research, are triggered by positive emotions. Positive emotions lead us to explore, connect, learn and expand our resourcefulness, which in turn makes our lives better, giving us further opportunities to experience positive emotions, and so on. This is exciting if you think of the potential when working with children. Whether you work with a child who feels generally happy and satisfied, or one who feels unhappy and dissatisfied with life, they can still grow and thrive, and experience much enjoyment.

The overall theory underpinning these findings is Fredrickson's (2001) *Broaden and Build Theory of Positive Emotions* (BBT). Fredrickson's research indicates that positive emotions broaden our '*momentary thought–action repertoires*' (p.220) – the range of thoughts and actions we are willing and able to consider in the short term, including our ability to spot opportunities and focus our attention on situations and objects – whilst also building long-term resources such as resilience. Additionally, according to Fredrickson's BBT, positive emotions can 'correct or undo the after effects of negative emotions' (p.221). There is a growing body of evidence to suggest that positive emotions may be good for our health, by providing some protection from the negative impact that persistent negative emotions, such as anxiety and anger, have on our cardiovascular system (Tugade, Fredrickson and Barrett 2004).

This research also indicates that *emotional granularity* – the ability to clearly identify and express different emotions and their intensity – is important.

Based on the definitions of happiness and the effects of positive emotions described above, it is therefore a good idea to deliberately increase the ratio of positive emotions to negative ones, in order to increase happiness, resilience and overall wellbeing.

This doesn't mean that negative emotions should be ignored – they are a healthy part of the human emotional range. Someone feeling grief, or anger, can't simply wish it away by superimposing artificial positive emotions, nor should they. We can, however, build activities into our lives that allow us to feel more positive than negative emotions, such as pursuing hobbies we enjoy, watching comedy, listening to music, dancing, or learning new things. The list is endless, as we each have individual positive emotion triggers. One way to increase positive emotions is to have close friendships. According to Demır and Weitekamp (2007), the *quality* of our friendships is a strong predictor of happiness – more so than our personality or the number of friends we have. Delle Fave *et al.* (2011) confirm that it is important for our wellbeing to have close family/home relationships and a close circle of friends but, worryingly, also find that Western society increasingly places less value on wider social and community concerns. They say this challenge will need to be addressed by professionals and researchers alike, 'particularly when developing interventions targeting youth, education systems and policy makers' (p.204). Activities that target this aspect can be found in Chapters 1, 2, 3 and 9.

Will it always work?

We've seen earlier in this chapter that defining happiness is difficult. Children may struggle to think of themselves as 'happy'. We have therefore focused our activities mainly on the expression of the full range and intensity of emotion (granularity) and helping children experience more positive than negative emotions, as this still addresses happiness without an overt focus on it or its definition. Another way to overcome a child's difficulty around the theme of happiness is to focus the child on kindness activities first, which take the focus away from the child and place it on other people. This not only holds value from a moral perspective, but also enhances the child's wellbeing, as we have shown in Chapter 2.

There is evidence (Mauss *et al.* 2011) that the pursuit of happiness itself may lead to unhappiness, particularly in situations where someone would expect to feel happy (e.g. when celebrating a birthday or achievement) and consequently feels disappointed with themselves if they don't. This is another reason why we have focused the activities in this chapter on *emotions* as a means to increase happiness.

Emotions can be challenging for children to identify and express in words. This is why they can often erupt into physical manifestations, such as aggression, hyperactivity or withdrawal. In order to overcome this challenge, we have to teach children the vocabulary of emotions. We have provided some activities to do this under 'Emotional Granularity' (6.2).

6.1 EXPERIENCING POSITIVE EMOTIONS

6.1.1 I've got the giggles

- **Recommended age**

  5+ (for the younger age groups, do this as a spoken activity instead of a written one)

- **Duration**

  20 minutes

- **Resources**

  » Paper

  » Pens

- **Method**

  Have a brief class discussion about laughter. For example, ask a few pupils to tell the class the last time they laughed, and what made them laugh. Ask them how often they laughed in the last day, and the last week.

  Then give your pupils the following instructions:

  Write about something that always makes you laugh, or something that made you laugh in the last week.

  1. *What is it?*

  2. *Why does/did it make you laugh?*

  3. *When is the last time you laughed because of this?*

  4. *How does laughing make you feel?*

  Question 4 addresses emotional granularity – the ability to clearly express the emotions and their intensity – and may be too challenging for most of the children at the younger end of the age range. You may also find it easier to do this activity once you have done some work with the children to expand their emotional vocabulary (see the 'Emotional Granularity' activities, 6.2).

6.1.2 Feel-good playlist

- **Recommended age**

  5+

- **Duration**

  15 minutes

- **Resources**

  » Recorded music/songs and the means to play them through loudspeakers in class

- **Method**

  Ask the children what songs make them feel good. Compile a playlist that you can then play as background music during lessons at appropriate times.

6.1.3 Feel-good planner

This activity teaches children that it is possible to deliberately do things that make them feel good, every day.

- **Recommended age**

  8+

- **Duration**

  8 days in total: Day 0 is preparation day (allow 15–30 minutes, depending on whether the children draw their own tables or you provide them as a handout), then 10 minutes per day on Days 1–7

- **Resources**

  » Pens

  » Paper

- **Method**

  The children will need a sheet of paper each, with a table containing, across the top, column headings: *Day 1, Day 2, Day 3*, etc. (through to *Day 7*). On the left of the table, have the following row headings:

  Activity

  How long will it take?

  Best time of day to do it?

  How did it make you feel?

They can create the table themselves, copying from an example on the board, or you can provide them with a handout already containing the table.

The last question addresses emotional granularity – the ability to clearly express the emotions and their intensity. You may find it easier to do this activity once you have done some of the activities in 'Emotional Granularity' (6.2).

Allow enough space in the last row for pupils to describe how the activity made them feel, physically and emotionally. You may need to help them by drawing out relevant vocabulary with them.

Now pupils need to decide what activities they are going to do. They need to have a different activity for Days 1–7. They then write this into the 'Activity' row of the table.

During these seven days, the children need to do the activity (inside or outside of school) for each day, and you will need to allow time in class for them to complete the table. Remind them on the Friday afternoon that they will need to complete their activities and fill in the table at the weekend as homework. To ensure pupils are familiar with what they need to do, we advise starting this activity early in the week.

6.1.4 Best possible self (BPS)

Research (Layous, Nelson and Lyubomirsky 2013; Sheldon and Lyubomirsky 2006) shows that BPS activities improve mood in the short term (i.e. create positive emotions). Layous *et al.* (2013) also found that the positive impact is greater if those doing the activity are told, before they do it, that the activity will make them feel great.

● **Recommended age**

8+

● **Duration**

30 minutes

- **Resources**

  » Pens, including felt-tip pens/crayons/coloured pencils

  » Paper

- **Method**

  Ask pupils to spend some time imagining their future. You can let them decide which point in the future they want to take themselves to or give them a specific point (e.g. 'five years from today').

  Tell them they need to think of their future in the present tense (i.e. as if they were at that point in time and living it, right now). Ask them to imagine that everything has gone exactly the way they wanted it to, in every aspect of their lives, and to think beyond school/career. Encourage them to think about the kind of life they want to live and the kind of person they want to be.

  They need to write down their vision of their BPS on their pieces of paper, and can include colours or drawings if they wish. The writing can be in bullet point form, or prose, or by way of a mind map. It is their BPS and they can represent and visualise it in whichever way works for them.

6.2 EMOTIONAL GRANULARITY

Teaching children the language of emotions is a key factor in enhancing their emotional granularity – their ability to express what they feel, and how intensely they feel it. It is also a great way to improve their verbal and written communication skills, so can be used to complement the English Language curriculum.

We recently discovered a great tool to help with this: 'My Feelings Box' by Feeling Magnets,[1] which come with their own activity suggestions on the Emotion Superpower[2] website; their 'What am I feeling?' page[3] is also worth a visit, as it has a very simple, clear and

---

1 www.feelingmagnets.com
2 www.emotionsuperpower.com
3 www.emotionsuperpower.com/what

free step-by-step guide to help children explore their emotions. You can use the website to familiarise yourself with the vocabulary and strategies and/or let individual children work their way through the options under your supervision. There are, of course, other products, such as cards and games, to help children develop their emotional vocabulary. You may also find the 'Feelings Inventory' on the 'Center for Nonviolent Communication' website[4] useful.

When you do the suggested classroom activities, below, with children, focus on the development of a wide range and strength of emotional vocabulary. So, rather than 'very sad', are they 'miserable', for example? And rather than 'really excited', might they be 'curious', 'playful', 'hopeful'?

Explore the language and its meanings with them to enrich their vocabulary and ability to express how they feel.

Displaying emotional vocabulary around the classroom, perhaps colour-coded by category of emotion, will help pupils choose appropriate words during the activities.

You could also use these activities to help children prepare for the 'My mood' activity (5.1.5).

6.2.1 'Inside out'

• Recommended age

5+ (the depth of understanding, and the level of discussion, will vary depending on the age and maturity of the children)

• Duration

120–180 minutes (you will likely need to split this over a number of sessions, to fit in with your timetable, and also the attention span of the children – use your judgement regarding the latter, based on the age and maturity of your pupils)

---

4   www.cnvc.org/Training/feelings-inventory

- **Resources**

  - » DVD of the film *Inside Out* (Rivera and Docter 2015)

  - » Pens

  - » Paper

- **Method**

  Watch (or re-watch!) the film and familiarise yourself with the concepts, characters and storyline. Plan preparatory and follow-up questions that are appropriate to the age and maturity of the children you are working with.

  Tell the children you are going to watch the Disney Pixar film *Inside Out* and that you want them to pay particular attention to the emotions, and jot down thoughts they have about things such as whether they recognise any of the emotions in themselves, whether they can think of times when they've heard their own *inner voice* talking to them, why particular scenes make them laugh (or cry), etc.

  After you have watched the film, have a further discussion: split the class into smaller groups and give each group one or two questions to discuss, then mix up the groups so that you have at least one person from each initial group in each new group and they can share what they discussed in their first groups (see also the 'Co-operative learning' activity, 9.1.6).

  You may want to include questions such as:

  - » *How many different emotions were there in the film?*

  - » *What job (purpose) did each emotion have?*

  - » *Was any one emotion more important than the others?*

  - » *Why/why not? How can you tell how someone is feeling?*

  - » *How do you act when you are feeling sad/angry/happy?*

  - » *Is it OK to feel sad/angry? Why/why not?*

If you search for *Inside Out* lesson plans or charts online, you will find a wealth of resources you can use in your lessons. Pinterest, in particular, has some great charts.

6.2.2 Happy song, sad song

* **Recommended age**

  8+

* **Duration**

  10 minutes

* **Resources**

  » Two songs – one 'sad', one 'happy' – and the means to play them in class over a loudspeaker

* **Method**

  Play a 'sad' song to the class. Choose one that is quite obviously sad based on tempo, musical tone and lyrics.

  Ask children how the song made them feel, using as wide a range of emotional vocabulary as possible.

  Repeat the activity with a 'happy' song.

6.2.3 A perfect day

* **Recommended age**

  10+

* **Duration**

  20 minutes

- **Resources**

  » Paper

  » Pens

- **Method**

  Ask the pupils to imagine a perfect day. Here is some suggested wording for the instructions:

  > *Imagine a perfect day. Think about what you would do, who you would see, where you would go. What would the weather be like? What would you eat and drink? What would you wear? Really visualise the day as if you were there.*

  > *Now think about your feelings. How are you feeling on this perfect day? Think about the words we have been working on that describe feelings, and which ones describe your feelings best.*

  > *Write your story down in as much detail as possible.*

6.2.4 Pictures of fun

- **Recommended age**

  8+

- **Duration**

  30 minutes

- **Resources**

  » Paper

  » Pens for writing, and felt-tip pens/crayons/coloured pencils for drawing

- **Method**

Ask the children to draw three pictures to represent the three activities they love doing the most (e.g. a sports activity, playing with friends, playing an instrument, cooking, etc.).

Ask them to write under each picture some words to describe how they feel when they do that activity, taking care to use the most accurate words for their emotions.

6.2.5 Feel-good planner – extension activity

- **Recommended age**

8–11

- **Duration**

15 minutes

- **Resources**

  » Pens

  » Paper (ideally use the back of the completed 'feel-good planner')

- **Method**

After the children have done the 'Feel-good planner' activity (6.1.3), give them the following questions to answer, in writing:

1. *Which were your three favourite activities of the week?*

2. *Why did you pick those three?*

3. *Write in more detail (one to two sentences for each activity) how you felt during and after each activity.*

6.2.6 Best possible self (BPS) – extension activity

- **Recommended age**

  8+

- **Duration**

  10 minutes

- **Resources**

  » None

- **Method**

  After completing the 'BPS' activity (6.1.4), pair pupils up to discuss how it felt to do the activity and how they feel now, having completed it. As with all activities in this section, encourage and support them in using the specific emotional vocabulary.

6.2.7 Feelings poster

This activity may be easier to do after having done the 'Feel-good planner' activity (6.1.3), 'I've got the giggles' activity (6.1.1), and/or 'Pictures of fun' activity (6.2.4). Because of its collaborative nature, this activity also promotes teamwork and positive relationships (see Chapters 3 and 9, respectively).

- **Recommended age**

  8+

- **Duration**

  Up to 2 hours (you can split this over a number of lessons/days)

- **Resources**

  » Poster paper

  » Smaller paper, in various colours

  » Colouring pencils/crayons/felt-tip pens

  » Glue

  » Space on a wall to display the poster

- **Method**

  Have a whole class brainstorm to come up with as many words as possible to describe a wide range of emotions, and write them on a board or flipchart. Once you have a decent list (try to have it more or less evenly balanced between 'positive' and 'negative' emotions), discuss as a whole class which of the emotions make you feel good, and which ones make you feel bad, and categorise the emotions on the board/flipchart accordingly.

  Next, discuss what activities you can do to make you feel good, and list these on the board/flipchart.

  As a class, you are now going to make a poster with the information you have gathered. Allocate a part of the poster to each child (i.e. an emotion or an activity to create positive emotions) and ask them to write it on a colourful piece of paper, and to decorate the paper however they wish, in a way that matches the activity or emotion.

  You will then create a large display poster with three headings: '*Words to describe emotions that feel good*', '*Words to describe emotions that feel bad*', '*Activities that make you feel good*', by attaching the pieces of paper the children have worked on individually.

6.3 WHOLE SCHOOL ACTIVITIES

Thanks to emotional contagion (Hatfield, Cacioppo and Rapson 1993), it is relatively easy to spread positive emotions across the whole school community once you start working on these in lessons and with individuals. You can, however, also build in whole school activities to help the process along.

6.3.1 Emotions assembly

For one assembly a week, or even at the start of each assembly, have a few volunteers (staff and children) tell a positive story about something that has happened to them recently that made them feel good. Ask them to share not only what happened but also how it felt, using the vocabulary of emotions they are getting increasingly familiar with.

6.3.2 Smile day

Have a designated day (and repeat this as often as you wish) where everyone smiles at everyone they meet as they walk through school. It is important to highlight that some people may not feel like smiling back, for reasons of their own (e.g. they may be grieving or struggling with something else that means they don't feel like smiling that day). This is OK, and nobody should be forced to initiate smiles, either. This activity should, however, encourage the majority of the school community to share smiles on a designated day, and may cause ripples of increased smiles, and their emotionally uplifting effects, all year round.

6.3.3 Emotional temperature

You can take the daily emotional 'temperature' of the school, by having two clear, see-through boxes or buckets displayed prominently in reception, and a basket full of tokens of some kind to use as counters, as well as a poster explaining the purpose of the activity and how it works.

As everyone (staff, pupils, parents, visitors) walks in each day, they take a token and put it into the 'I feel good' box/bucket, or the 'I feel "meh"' box/bucket. Each box/bucket could also have a simple picture: a smiling face for the 'good' box and a frowning face for the 'meh' box.

The activity requires minimal management. Each day, it is easily visible to all whether the positive emotions or negative emotions side has more tokens. At the end of each day, a designated member of the administration team can log this in a spreadsheet before emptying the boxes back into the token basket, to start again the next day. As this 'temperature' is being logged each day, you can then look at trends over a period of time. You may even notice that there are more positive days once the culture of positive emotions has become firmly embedded in your school!

Chapter 7

MINDFULNESS AND MEDITATION

Mindfulness is an ancient pursuit stemmed in Buddhist practice and philosophy. Only recently science has begun catching up with the impact that mindfulness can have on individuals, and the wider community, and not just from a spiritual perspective. So what, exactly, is mindfulness?

Mindfulness is being wholly present in any given moment, and through being present, cultivating an awareness of thought, action, feeling and context, without judgement. Being actively mindful on a day-to-day basis is extremely hard and it 'does not come naturally to most people' (Zerbo *et al.* 2016, p.3), though with consistent practice, generally over an eight-week programme (we recommend going beyond eight weeks with your class and making it an ongoing practice), there are significant benefits. Research shows that there is a reduction in anxiety and depressive symptoms, an increase in focus and emotion-regulation (Freudenthaler, Turba and Tran 2017), and significant increases in self-esteem, resilience and happiness (Yook, Kang and Park 2017).

Mindfulness and meditation are closely related practices. Mindfulness is typically developed by using different individual or group meditation techniques and can either be self-directed or guided. Mindfulness meditation techniques include: mindful meditation, walking meditation, mindful eating, and body scan.

Because these two practices are so intricately linked, we have covered them under one chapter.

Meditation is the practice of focusing on one thing (attention training). Its benefits include many of the benefits of mindfulness, in addition to a decrease in mind wandering (Jazaieri *et al.* 2016), an increase in compassionate behaviours, and the lowering of stress levels (Yoo *et al.* 2016).

When planning to incorporate mindfulness and meditation activities into your classroom, be mindful (pun intended!) of the age and attention span of your class. We recommend that you start with short activities, gradually increasing the time, based on how your pupils respond. The times we have indicated for each activity can be lengthened accordingly.

Will it always work?

Mindfulness and meditation can be a relatively easy way to bring more focus, gratitude and happiness into life, but some people struggle with it. If a child you are working with declares that they cannot focus, that they are bored, or that they don't like the thoughts that arise during a mindfulness and meditation exercise, perhaps consider doing more active and thought-provoking exercises. You could, for example, stick with the 'Mindful colouring' activity (7.2.2), or encourage them to go for a walk with the aim of noticing certain things in nature (see the 'Take a walk' activity, 7.2.3). There are ways to surreptitiously increase focus and counteract potential boredom and/or dissatisfaction with meditation and mindfulness activities.

At the International Positive Psychology Association (IPPA) World Congress 2017, Sharon Salzberg[1] and Barbara Fredrickson[2] ran a joint presentation session (Fredrickson and Salzberg 2017) about *loving kindness meditation* (see the 'Loving kindness meditation' activity, 7.1.5). During her presentation, Salzberg stated

---

1   www.sharonsalzberg.com
2   www.positiveemotions.org

that people often say they tried mindfulness and it didn't work, but according to her, this is because of preconceptions, such as the necessity to have a clear mind, or to think only happy thoughts, or not to feel sleepy. According to Salzberg, however, 'you cannot fail at mindfulness' (Fredrickson and Salzberg 2017), as it is about really paying attention and making considered choices. Explaining this to children who struggle with these practices may help them put less pressure on themselves and enjoy the process.

Another way to help your meditations run smoothly is to set a calm environment as you start a meditation, for example by changing your voice to a soft, soothing tone. We recommend, if you are not familiar with the practice of meditation, that you try some meditations yourself first, so that you are familiar and comfortable with the process, as well as the appropriate tonality and volume of your voice. You can do this by searching for guided meditations on YouTube, and there are some excellent 'apps' for your phone that you can download and use for free initially, such as 'Headspace' and 'Calm'.

▓ 7.1 MIND THAT BREATH ▓

This set of activities will provide you with simple guided breath and body meditations. These activities will be useful in class, particularly when you want to calm your pupils down after lunch breaks or sports. Guided meditation and focus on their breath and/or body will help them mentally come back into the room and into a space of focus and self-regulation. The activities will start with the easiest guided meditation first, and increase in complexity of focus as you increase your confidence in guiding a meditation and your pupils' skills grow.

With all breathing meditations, it is important for pupils to breathe properly 'into their bellies'. This is called diaphragmatic breathing/ abdominal breathing (Guy's and St Thomas' NHS Foundation Trust 2016) and is where we push the diaphragm down to allow our lungs to fully expand as they take in air and, as a result, our abdomen expands as our abdominal contents are pushed downwards and outwards.

Children – and adults – often initially struggle to feel the abdominal rise and fall that we describe in the exercises. To help them, get them to lie down flat on their backs (or ask them to do this at home) and breathe normally, with their hands gently resting on their abdomens. When lying on our backs, we automatically breathe abdominally, so this allows the children to tune in to what it feels like.

7.1.1 'Take five' meditation

This meditation is one frequently used with young children as it is so simple to teach and do.

- **Recommended age**

  5–11

- **Duration**

  30–40 seconds

- **Resources**

  » None

- **Method**

  Ensure the children are sitting comfortably in their chairs, with their backs upright, their feet on the floor, hip-width apart, and their shoulders relaxed. It may help to ask them to gently wriggle their shoulders to ensure they're relaxed.

  Demonstrate the meditation activity first, then ask the children to do it. Here are some suggested instruction words for you to use with the children:

  1. *Hold one hand in front of your chest, with your fingers outstretched and slightly apart.*

  2. *Now close your eyes.*

3. *With your other hand, start tracing the fingers of your outstretched hand, beginning at the base of your thumb.*

4. *Trace each finger slowly, breathing in as you move up the finger, and breathing out as you move back down the other side of your finger. Start with your thumb, then continue with your index finger, your middle finger, your ring finger and, finally, your little finger.*

5. *As you trace each finger, focus on how your breath feels as it comes in and out of your body. Feel yourself relaxing with each breath, and also notice the sensations on your hand as you gently trace each finger.*

N.B. This activity can be done with eyes either open or closed. When doing it with eyes closed, it's great to focus on the physical sensation of the finger tracing each finger in the outstretched hand. When doing it with eyes open, the child can focus their visual attention on the action of tracing each finger. The act of paying attention to this one action is really important to ensure they stay focused and avoid being distracted by external stimuli.

Demonstrate a slow pace of breathing as you show the children the exercise, and until they are used to it, guide them through it by giving gentle vocal cues of 'In' and 'Out' as they move up and down each finger.

This activity can, of course, be repeated more than once for a longer meditation, and once children are familiar with it, you can also use it with individual children if they need to refocus on an activity, or calm down in a potential conflict/anger situation. Simply gently saying to the child 'Take five', or holding your hand up with fingers splayed and stretched, should be enough to signal to them that it would be a good idea for them to do this simple meditation. The child can then do the meditation there and then, sitting or standing. If standing, we recommend the child's eyes stay open to avoid falling over!

▨ 7.1.2 Mindful breathing

- **Recommended age**

  8+

- **Duration**

  1–5 minutes

- **Resources**

  » Space for every child to sit or lie down comfortably

  » If you wish, you can use a bell or similar instrument, such as a triangle or Tibetan singing bowl

- **Method**

  Ask the children to sit in their chairs, or lie on a suitable mat, in a comfortable position, with their hands gently resting on their bellies. Explain to them that as a class you are all going to close your eyes, and you will guide them through a breathing exercise. Ask everyone to remain as still and silent as they can. To start the meditation exercise, if you choose to, you can ring a bell (or triangle, etc.). Below is a suggested script for your guided meditation, but you can, of course, create your own:

  > *With your eyes closed, and your hands on your belly, start noticing your breath. Notice how, as you breathe in and out, and your lungs fill and empty, your belly goes up and down. Focus on this feeling for a moment...*

  Stay silent for 15–30 seconds – you can increase the duration of your silence as pupils become more practised at this activity.

  > *Now we are going to take some really big, deep breaths, and pay attention to what that feels like. I am going to count five breaths with you, so when I say 'One', you take one big slow deep breath*

and let it out. And again when I say 'Two', take another big slow deep breath and let it out, and so on... Ready... One...

Give them all time to take a deep, slow breath in, and out.

... Two... Three... Four... Five...

You can repeat these steps a couple of times, encouraging the children to mentally count the breaths, so they can do the activity in silence.

Now do this again, but count silently in your head as you breathe in and out. Remember to focus on how your breath feels. When you get to 'Five', gently open your eyes as you breathe out, then stretch.

If you are guiding them through the counting, you need to end the activity for them. You can use whichever instrument/chime you used to start the activity to draw the activity to a close, or you can simply ask your pupils to open their eyes and have a stretch (a stretch is a good way to bring movement and blood flow back into their muscles, and to 'wake them up' after the relaxing activity).

7.1.3 Thought bubbles

● **Recommended age**

8+

● **Duration**

3+ minutes

● **Resources**

» Space for children to sit or lie comfortably

» If you wish, you can use a bell or similar instrument, such as a triangle or Tibetan singing bowl

- **Method**

  Ask the children to sit comfortably in their chairs, or provide enough space for them to lie down. Explain to them that as a class you are all going to close your eyes, and you will guide them through a breathing exercise. Ask everyone to remain as still and silent as they can. You may wish to ring a bell (or triangle, etc.) to signify the start of the exercise, but this is not essential. Below is a suggested script for your guided meditation:

  > *With your eyes closed, and your hands on your belly, notice your breath. Notice how, as you breathe in and out and your lungs fill and empty, your belly goes up and down. Focus on this feeling for a moment...*

  Stay silent for a minute or so.

  > *Now we are going to take some really big, deep breaths, and pay attention to what that feels like. I am going to count five breaths with you, so when I say 'One', you take one big slow deep breath and let it out, and again when I say 'Two', you take another big slow deep breath and let it out, and so on... Ready... One...*

  Give them all time to take a deep, slow breath in, and out.

  > *... Two... Three... Four... Five...*

  Count their breaths two or three times and then move onto the next part of the activity.

  > *Now that you are comfortable with your breath, we are going to observe our thoughts. As thoughts pop into your head, instead of grabbing hold of them and focusing on them, imagine they are turning into bubbles. As each thought appears, watch it turn into a bubble, then float into the air, and away.*
  >
  > *Let's spend a minute or two watching our thoughts become bubbles and float away...*

  Give them a few minutes to observe their breath and thoughts. If you are using a bell, you can ring it to draw the activity to a close, or you can simply ask your pupils to open their eyes and have a stretch (a stretch is a good way to bring movement and blood flow back into their muscles, and to 'wake them up' after the relaxing activity).

7.1.4 In the body scanner

* **Recommended age**

  8+

* **Duration**

  5 minutes

* **Resources**

  » Space for children to sit or lie comfortably

  » If you wish, you can use a bell or similar instrument, such as a triangle or Tibetan singing bowl

* **Method**

  Ask the children to sit comfortably in their chairs or provide enough space for them to lie down. Explain to them that as a class you are all going to close your eyes, and you will guide them through a body scanning exercise. Ask everyone to remain as still and silent as they can. Tell your pupils to imagine that their mind is a body scanner and after they have checked in on their breathing, they are going to use their mind to check in on how their body feels, to see if they feel relaxed, tired, jittery, tense, hot, cold, and so on. You may wish to ring a bell (or triangle, etc.) to signify the start of the exercise, but this is not essential. Below is a suggested script for your guided meditation:

  > *With your eyes closed, and your hands on our belly, notice your breath. Notice how, as you breathe in and out and your lungs fill and empty, your belly goes up and down. Focus on this feeling for a moment...*

Stay silent for a minute or so.

> *Now we are going to take some really big, deep, slow breaths, and notice what that feels like. I am going to count five breaths with you, so when I say 'One' you take one big deep breath and let it out, and again when I say 'Two', you take one big deep breath and let it out, and so on... Ready... One...*

Give them all time to take a deep, slow breath in and out.

> *... Two... Three... Four... Five...*

Count their breaths two or three times, then move on to the next part of the activity.

> *Now we are going to scan down our bodies – imagine the scanner as a coloured light that is moving down from your head to your feet, and it is sending back information to you about how your body feels. So, starting at the top of your head, activate your coloured light scanner and start moving it down your head and face...*

Give the pupils an appropriate amount of time here to comfortably scan down their heads and faces – be aware of timing throughout the whole exercise.

> *... Notice any tightness, any relaxed muscles, any itchiness, or coldness, and let it go... Now scan down your neck and into your shoulders, again noticing what they feel like... Scan down your arms, right down to the tips of your fingers... Now scan your torso, your chest and lungs, down your tummy and back. Is there any tension there? Any sore muscles? Whatever you notice, acknowledge it, then let it go and keep on scanning... Now scan down your legs, down to your knees, calves, and right into your littlest toe.*

If you are using a bell, you can ring it to draw the activity to a close, or you can simply ask your pupils to open their eyes and have a stretch (a stretch is a good way to bring movement and blood flow back into their muscles, and to 'wake them up' after the relaxing activity).

▨ 7.1.5 Loving kindness meditation

This is a beautiful meditation, but some people struggle with it, sometimes because they find it difficult to be kind to themselves, which is why it may be useful to start this activity by projecting *loving kindness* to other people. According to Salzberg (Fredrickson and Salzberg 2017), the original term for this meditation is *metta*, for which the literal translation is *friendship*, but she feels that isn't exactly the right word, either. She describes *loving kindness* as breaking down the barriers that prevent us wishing someone well, but without any implication regarding how we spend our time. Salzberg explains that it is possible to feel loving kindness towards someone without it being appropriate to spend time with that person (e.g. a person who drains our energy and makes us feel bad about ourselves). She uses the word *connection*, as it doesn't imply you have to like the person. Loving kindness meditation is therefore a powerful tool to bring us a sense of peace, especially if we are able to extend it to people we don't know, or know and don't like.

Below, we describe our version of the loving kindness meditation.

- **Recommended age**

  10+

- **Duration**

  2–10 minutes

- **Resources**

  » A quiet space for children (or child if done on an individual basis) to sit comfortably

- **Method**

  Ask your pupils to close their eyes and think of someone whom they really care about, whom they love. This could be a family member or a friend or even the family pet. Ask them to think about what makes this person special to them. Next, ask your pupils to close their eyes and hold their hands over their heart while they picture this person in their mind. Here are some suggested words:

Imagine your special person, what they look like, including the clothes that they wear, and their face. Think about how lovely it feels to hug this person and to see them happy. Imagine this special person doing something they love to do. Do they like to cook, or draw, or play a sport? I want you to imagine that, as they are doing what they love, you are walking up to them and giving them a hug filled with huge amounts of love. Imagine all of that love gathering in your heart... You are now going to release that love and send it out towards that special person.

Once the pupils have sent out this feeling of love, invite them to say: 'May you be happy, healthy and strong.' This is our suggested wording, but you can adapt this or even encourage children to come up with their own. Salzberg's (Fredrickson and Salzberg 2017) wording is: 'May you be safe, may you be happy, may you be healthy, may you live with ease.' Allow pupils to have a few moments of quietness with their eyes still closed, then invite them to open their eyes, and ask them to share how the exercise made them feel.

Extension 1

As an extension of this exercise, before asking the children to open their eyes, ask them to remember what that love felt like when remembering their special person, and ask them to send that love to themselves. This could be a little hard for younger pupils to grasp, so use your judgement, and if you feel they will benefit, give it a go. Some suggested wording is:

Imagine that feeling of love and happiness that you felt for that special person. I want you now to gather that feeling again in your heart, and then send that love to yourself. Imagine it is going on a journey, from your heart to your head. I want you to now say: 'May I be happy, healthy and strong.'

After completing the extension, ask the pupils how it made them feel to send love to themselves.

Extension 2

You can further extend this exercise by encouraging pupils to extend their loving kindness meditation to:

» A person they know but don't have particularly strong positive or negative feelings towards. This could be a shop assistant they see regularly, for example.

» Someone who makes them smile and feel good. It doesn't have to be someone they personally know – it could be a role model.

» The whole school community.

» Their entire family.

» The whole world.

» Someone they don't like, or someone they've have had a row with. This one, along with the loving kindness towards oneself, is one of the hardest for people to do, but it can be made easier by explaining the definition of *loving kindness* as *connection*, as described by Salzberg (Fredrickson and Salzberg 2017) and mentioned in the introduction to this activity.

Again, at the end, ask the pupils how the activity made them feel. As a further note, it is not necessary to do this meditation in one sitting. It can be broken up into chunks to do at different times, if you wish to extend it to all the different people mentioned above. You can also encourage children simply to send the loving kindness thoughts to people as they go through their day. For example, as they walk past a teacher or friend in a corridor, they can simply mentally direct the loving kindness meditation words towards the person they just walked past.

▪ 7.2 GETTING OUT AND ABOUT

Mindfulness isn't only cultivated through meditation. There are other fun and interesting ways to bring your pupils back to the present moment and help them build awareness of the world around them. Developing their awareness of the world around them can open their minds.

▪ 7.2.1 Spider senses

- **Recommended age**

  5+

- **Duration**

  2–3 minutes

- **Resources**

  » None

- **Method**

  Spider senses is an activity to teach children to pause wherever they are and notice everything around them. When introducing this activity for the first time, explain to your class that their spider senses allow them to stop moving and notice what is around them and how it feels, so they notice what they can hear, see, smell, taste, feel on their skin, and so on. Explain that whenever you ask them to turn on their spider senses, you want them to pay attention to everything listed above. You can do this for an individual child or for a whole class. Give them a minute or so to 'sense' everything and then ask them what they experienced. Some suggested wording is below:

  [Child's name]... Pause and turn on your spider senses...

Let the child 'sense'.

> ... *What did you notice with your spider senses and how did it make you feel?*

If a child struggles with the exercise, take part yourself. Tune into your spider senses and discuss with the child what you both picked up on and how it made you feel.

7.2.2 Mindful colouring

This activity, like '"Take five" meditation' (7.1.1) and 'Mindful breathing' (7.1.2), is great to use as a calming activity after breaks or more boisterous times in class.

- **Recommended age**

  5+

- **Duration**

  5+ minutes

- **Resources**

  » Photocopies of line drawings (you can decide the complexity that your pupils can work with – perhaps for an older age group more complex patterns and illustrations will engage them more)

  » Coloured pencils, pens, crayons, etc.

- **Method**

  This is a great activity that can be used for the whole class. You can provide any type of picture for pupils to colour in, or themed pictures (e.g. to tie in with a particular time of year or holiday season, or to take the activity across the curriculum by giving them pictures to colour in related to topics and subjects they are learning about in science, art or English).

Hand out the pictures and colouring utensils and ask your pupils to remain silent whilst colouring in – the aim is for them to focus on the activity. Set them a time limit. They don't have to finish colouring in the picture, as they can come back to it during a later session, but if they know how long they have to focus for, this can help them to concentrate.

7.2.3 Take a walk

- **Recommended age**

  8+

- **Duration**

  10–20 minutes

- **Resources**

  » None

- **Method**

  Take your pupils out into the playground; or if your school premises include a wood or other green space, take them there. As you walk around the outdoor space, spend a minute or two getting them to focus on their breath (use the 'Mindful breathing' activity, 7.1.2, as a guide). Once they have settled into a mindful space, tell them they will now focus on what they can hear, see, smell, taste, feel on their skin, and so on. Ask them to tune into what else they can sense around them. Here are some suggested questions:

  » *Can you feel the breeze and/or the sun on your skin?*

  » *Can you feel the cement or the grass under your feet?*

  » *What do the trees sound like?*

  » *What do the clouds look like?*

» *Is it a warm or cold day?*

» *What do you hear?*

» *What do you feel?*

» *What do you see?*

Participate and engage with your pupils; this exercise is good for you as well, and the shared participation will help the class to bond. This activity can be a simple, quick way to calm your class down after a sports lesson, or at the end of a lunch break, or it could be a longer, more in-depth exploration of the world around them.

7.2.4 Leafy green

- **Recommended age**

  10+

- **Duration**

  5 minutes

- **Resources**

  » One fallen plant or tree leaf per pupil

- **Method**

  Hand out one leaf to each pupil. Ask them to sit quietly for five minutes, simply observing the leaf. Ask your pupils to hold their leaves and notice colour, vein patterns, shapes, texture, smell, and anything else you or they might notice. This exercise is so simple and yet very effective to bring pupils into the present.

7.3 WHOLE SCHOOL ACTIVITIES

Creating a culture of mindfulness in your school will help you develop a good sense of wellbeing and resilience. All of the activities above can be adapted to be used with the whole school, but we have provided a few more to help you develop a culture of mindfulness in school.

7.3.1 Mindful bell

Use a bell or a chime (or you can download a chime sound onto a phone or laptop). Ask your pupils (and/or staff) to close their eyes and wait for the chime sound. When they hear the chime, all they have to do is listen intently until it fades and they can't hear it any more. At this point, they can open their eyes. This activity is quick, simple, and can be used in an assembly for a whole school approach to mindfulness, in individual classrooms, or even in the staffroom as a calming start to staff meetings.

7.3.2 Flickering candle

This is a common meditative exercise and can be used with an actual candle, or a video/moving image of a candle (other suggestions for a video/moving image are: a campfire, swirling patterns, gentle waves lapping onto a beach). Simply gaze at the centre of the image for a few minutes, acknowledging the thoughts that come and go, but maintaining the gaze on the image. This is another good activity for the whole school, as well as the staffroom.

7.3.3 One breath

This is a useful meditation exercise to teach to pupils and staff, and is one that can be used multiple times during the day. Explain to pupils and staff (whether at an assembly or staff meeting) that when we are feeling overwhelmed or anxious it is good to focus on the breath, and that even just focusing on one breath can help us be calmer and become more present. All you have to do is stop whatever you are doing and simply notice one breath, and focus on the feeling as you breathe in and then breathe out.

7.3.4 Mindfulness dots

Place coloured sticker dots around the school. Explain to the children that whenever they see a coloured dot, it is a reminder for them to stop for a moment and be mindful. Tell them that they can stop and do the 'One breath' activity (7.3.3), engage their 'Spider senses' (7.2.1), silently extend a 'Loving kindness' thought (see 'Loving kindness meditation', 7.1.5) to someone, or simply take note of how they are feeling, then move on. This is a great way to really engage the whole school in mindfulness, including all the staff and parents, as this can be explained to them at parents' evenings.

7.3.5 Stop for a mindful moment

Introduce a practice in school whereby at a specific signal, everyone stops what they're doing and does a quick breathing meditation. This could be the '"Take five" meditation' (7.1.1) for younger children, or the 'Mindful breathing' activity (7.1.2) for older children and adults. The signal could be a particular way of ringing the school bell for the whole school community (including any visitors on site at the time – of course, it would require a brief explanation to them, and there could be posters in reception to explain the practice, too) to meditate for a minute or so.

Alternatively, children could be given permission to initiate a whole class 'mindful moment' whenever they feel that there is too much noise or disruption going on. This would empower children to self-manage classroom behaviour and encourage them to really tap into the power of meditation and mindfulness in order to achieve focus and inner stillness. There could be an agreed signal or code word that any child can say in class to instantly initiate a 'mindful moment'. You will need to use your judgement and knowledge of your children to decide whether this is suitable for them and to set boundaries/rules with them about when it is appropriate to invoke a 'mindful moment'.

* * Chapter 8 *

PHYSICAL WELLBEING

Encouraging children to participate in regular sports activities, inside and outside of school, is important in order to help reduce obesity and sedentary living. Although one of us is a Paralympian, we are not sports coaches; our expertise lies in character and positive education, but we wanted to include some pointers to ensure you consider physical activity within the scope of character and positive education interventions, and have therefore included some simple activities to introduce movement into your pupils' (and your!) everyday lives.

The benefits of physical activity in relation to physical health are many and generally widely known. As this book is about the development of mental wellbeing through character and positive education, let's look at some of the benefits of exercise from this perspective.

Mental health

Numerous studies have been carried out into the effectiveness of exercise in both the treatment and prevention of mental illness. Fox (1999) has conducted an extensive narrative review and summary of research findings spanning some 15 years and concluded that exercise reduces anxiety and depression, increases self-esteem, and improves 'mental wellbeing in the general public' (p.411).

Edmunds, Biggs and Goldie (2013) support these findings and list numerous benefits, including the enhancement of positive moods, reduction of stress, and an increase in sociable behaviour.

Character

Lumpkin (2011) highlights the importance of the role of parents, teachers and coaches in taking sports as an opportunity to help children develop positive character traits. Whilst sports may not, per se, develop positive character traits, these can be a useful springboard for role-modelling and teaching these traits to children.

Positive motivation

Wright and Burton (2008) examined studies aimed at improving physical and mental wellbeing for disadvantaged youths in the USA. They found that certain activities, such as Tai Chi, generated conversations about mental health and positive relationships. They also cited extensive research showing that 'physical activity programs can contribute to a positive motivational climate, perceived autonomy, intrinsic motivation, and a variety of social skills' (p.139).

Will it always work?

Some children, even at a very young age, may have already developed a negative perception of sports and physical exercise. In order to help you overcome any reluctance on their part to participate, we have included activities that are so surreptitious that children may not even initially realise they are exercising! Additionally, we have aimed to keep these activities fun and lighthearted, to allow you to introduce movement through playfulness. As always, of course, not all activities work with all children, and it may be that you need to try activities from other chapters that include physical activity (e.g. 'Dance moves', 3.1.2).

■ 8.1 CLASS ACTIVITIES

■ 8.1.1 Sneaky squats

This activity is aimed at introducing very simple movement into the school day, to interrupt the sedentary nature of lessons. It is 'sneaky', because – at least the first time you do it – your pupils may not even realise that they are doing exercise.

- **Recommended age**

  5+

- **Duration**

  1 minute

- **Resources**

  » None

- **Method**

  Ask your pupils to put down pens and paper and stand up. Once they're up, ask them to sit back down again. Repeat. After three to four times, you can tell them that they've actually been doing squats. At this point, tell them you'll now be doing ten squats together. Join in with the children, as the squats will be good for you, too! Repeat this as often as needed throughout the day, if you feel pupils are getting lethargic or generally have been sitting for too long.

■ 8.1.2 Surreptitious stretches

This activity works in a similar way to the 'Sneaky squats' activity (8.1.1).

- **Recommended age**

  5+

- **Duration**

  2–3 minutes

- **Resources**

  » None

- **Method**

  Ask your pupils to put down their pens and put one hand up as if to ask a question. Then, once their hands are up, tell them to stretch upwards as if they're reaching for something, so they're stretching their arms upwards. Now repeat this with the other arm (at this point, it will no longer be surreptitious!). Next, ask them to repeat the process, but pointing each arm forwards, as if pushing something away. Next, ask them to stretch each arm sideways, as if they are leaning against a wall and trying to push away from it. Then, ask them to stretch both arms out to their sides with their thumbs pointing down, and gently push their arms back. Next, ask them to relax their arms and return them to their sides, then tilt their head sideways, so their left ear moves towards their left shoulder (ensure the head moves towards the shoulder and not the other way around), then bring their head back to the centre, and repeat on the right. Finally, ask pupils to stand up, lean forwards and touch their knees or toes (lean as far as is comfortable for them, while feeling a gentle stretch). Then, before they sit back down, get them to gently shake, in turn, their hands and their feet.

  You can encourage your pupils to do this independently whenever they feel they need to stretch out a little. Based on your knowledge of your own pupils and the potential for disruption to your lessons, decide which movements to encourage them to do of their own accord.

8.1.3 Taking stock

* **Recommended age**

  8+

* **Duration**

  10–15 (older children may do this faster than younger ones)

* **Resources**

  » Pens

  » Paper

* **Method**

  Ask pupils to consider their current level of physical activity by writing down the answers to these questions:

  » *How much time do you spend sitting/moving?*

  » *Do you want to move more?*

  » *What fun ways do you have of moving your body?*

  You can extend this activity, if you wish, by holding a small group or class discussion about their answers (including, possibly, demonstrations of physical activities) and additional questions, such as:

  » *Why is it important to move your body?*

  » *How much should you move your body each day?*

▨ 8.1.4 My healthy body

- **Recommended age**

  8+

- **Duration**

  20 minutes

- **Resources**

  » Pens, including felt-tip pens/crayons/coloured pencils

  » Paper

- **Method**

  Ask pupils to think about, and write down (or draw), three different ways to be physically active outside of traditional sports (i.e. how to integrate more activity into everyday life). Examples could include taking the stairs instead of the lift, walking or cycling to school instead of taking the bus or being driven in a car, skipping instead of walking. Let their imaginations run free!

▨ 8.1.5 Physically fit

This activity is aimed at encouraging children to develop good habits by incorporating movement into daily life.

- **Recommended age**

  8+

- **Duration**

  8 days in total: Day 0 is preparation day (allow 15–30 minutes, depending on whether the children draw their own tables or you provide them as a handout), then 5–10 minutes per day on Days 1–7

- **Resources**

  » Pens

  » Paper

- **Method**

  The children will need a sheet of paper each, with a table containing, across the top, column headings: *Day 1, Day 2, Day 3*, etc. (through to *Day 7*). On the left of the table, have the following row headings:

  Activity

  Tick once you've done it

  How long did you do it for?

  How did it make you feel?

  They can create the table themselves, copying from an example on the board, or you can provide them with a handout already containing the table.

  Allow enough space in the last row for pupils to describe how the activity made them feel, physically and emotionally. You may need to help them by drawing out relevant vocabulary with them (see the 'Emotional Granularity' activities, 6.2).

  Now pupils need to decide what activities they are going to do. They need to have a different activity for Days 1–7. They will now write this into the 'Activity' row of the table.

  During these seven days, they need to do the activity (inside or outside of school) they've written down for each day, and you will need to allow time in class for them to complete the table. Remind them on the Friday afternoon that they will need to complete their activities and fill in the table at the weekend as homework. To ensure pupils are familiar with what they need to do, we advise starting this activity early in the week.

8.2 WHOLE SCHOOL ACTIVITIES

8.2.1 Stop and stretch

This is a variation on the 'Surreptitious stretches' activity (8.1.2), and the 'Mindfulness dots' activity (7.3.4).

Put coloured dots in various places around the school. Each time someone (staff or pupil) walks past one of the 'stop and stretch' dots, they need to do a simple stretch, reaching up with both arms as far as they can. You can be a little creative with this and come up with your own stretch options that are safe and quick to do in a busy school environment.

8.2.2 Long way around

Using footprint cut-outs in different colours, you can indicate longer routes to and from key places in the school (e.g. office, hall, library). This is a very simple nudge (Halpern 2016) technique to influence behaviour and encourage more physical activity.

8.2.3 Keep track

Many children are now aware of, and use, activity trackers, but these can be prohibitively expensive. Your school leadership team could ask a local business to sponsor the school by providing a number of activity trackers. You could then invite pupils and staff to apply for a tracker, which would require them to commit to a certain daily activity level. You could also introduce an element of fun competitiveness to this, by having leaderboards.

Chapter 9

POSITIVE RELATIONSHIPS

Our relationships – the connection we have with other people – drive most of our emotions. Remember your best moment and worst moment from the last week. Chances are that both had something to do with your interaction with other people. Diener and Seligman's (2002) research indicates that the happiest people have the richest social relationships. Additionally, a meta-analysis by Wang, Wu and Liu (2003) found evidence that good levels of social support improve physical and mental wellbeing. Cohen *et al.* (1997) also found a link between social connection and health. Astonishingly, social connection has even been found to reduce our experience of pain (Eisenberger *et al.* 2011; Master *et al.* 2009).

Why do relationships matter in a school environment?
Resilience and wellbeing

In their 2017 position paper, Ungar *et al.* state that schools provide resilience-enhancing resources such as supportive relationships and social cohesion. Roffey (2012) highlights that, in order to promote psychological health, schools need to provide an environment that includes 'connectedness and caring relationships between all stakeholders' (p.147) as well as strong wider community links. According to McGrath and Noble (2010), for pupils to experience good physical and mental health, and enjoy successful relationships in later life, school peer relationships are highly important.

Academic attainment and learning engagement

Peer relationships have been linked to raised academic attainment (Cornelius-White 2007; Jackson and Sherriff 2013; McGrath and Noble 2010; Reynolds *et al.* 2017), as well as improved attendance at school (Cornelius-White 2007) and learning engagement (McGrath and Noble 2010). Belonging to a group (e.g. the school community) is seen as particularly important by Reynolds *et al.* (2017), who describe it as 'fundamental to academic success'. Additionally, Cornelius-White's (2007) meta-analysis points to the improvement in critical thinking, student participation and self-esteem as a result of positive pupil–teacher relationships.

Involvement of the wider community

Roffey (2012) states that the involvement of parents in supporting the work of teachers in school – with all stakeholders working towards a common goal, and particularly the focus on strong relationships between school and the wider community – is important. McCarthy and Vickers (2012) also support the importance of involving all groups representing the wider local community.

Will it always work?

Schools are reflections of the communities they are based in, so often any tensions present in a community can be found in its schools; but even in a very cohesive community, a school is a natural hub for separate groups – for example teachers, pupils and parents – to form. In 2004, Tajfel and Turner wrote about *social identity theory*, whereby we define our sense of who we are and the place we hold in society based on the various groups we belong to. Our sense of social identity is reinforced by our perception that our in-group (the group we belong to) is superior to relevant out-groups (groups that we don't belong to). Think about any conflict (e.g. in the workplace, between sports teams, between countries); there is always a sense of being on one side or the other, of in-groups versus out-groups. Schools are rife with multiple in- and out-groups.

In this context, it is always possible that some children will not wish to engage with certain activities from time to time. The activities in this chapter, however, are mostly designed in such a way that children have much choice in who to direct prosocial elements of particular tasks at, whilst still allowing everyone to feel included. As with all activities in this book, whilst we encourage you to give children an opportunity to step outside their comfort zones, pushing too much could be counter-productive. If a child refuses to engage, it may be worth trying to understand the emotions driving the refusal (see 'Emotional Granularity', 6.2) and perhaps considering a mindfulness or meditation activity (see Chapter 7) before re-attempting to engage the child in the original activity.

9.1 ACTIVITIES TO ENCOURAGE PROSOCIAL BEHAVIOURS

9.1.1 Helping my team

- **Recommended age**

  8+

- **Duration**

  30+ minutes

- **Resources**

  » Coloured pencils/crayons/felt-tip pens

  » Plain paper

- **Method**

  Discuss with pupils any teams that they are in (e.g. sports teams, choirs and school houses). Encourage them to think beyond traditional teams, too – for example, their friendship group, their family, their class, the school, and the wider school community, including parents, are all teams (see also the activities in Chapter 3, 'Teamwork').

  Once you have come up with a good range of teams, ask pupils to think about someone in one of their teams whom they have recently helped, or someone who might need help. Ask them to draw a picture of the person they have thought of, then write a few sentences under the picture or overleaf, to explain how they have helped that person, or how/why they would like to help that person.

  Extension/variation

  In order to use this activity in a cross-curricular way and cover aspects of writing in the English Language curriculum, you could ask pupils to use particular linguistic devices when they write the description. For example, you could encourage them to use adjectives to describe the person and the situation in as much detail as possible. You could also use this as a creative writing activity, where children imagine a situation where they are a hero helping out a person in need.

9.1.2 Make someone laugh

Provine (2000) stated that 'the critical stimulus for laughter is another person, not a joke' (p.58). This doesn't mean that jokes don't work, but it does mean that, at the heart of the success of a joke lies a connection between the person telling the joke and the person laughing (even if it is a professional connection, such as the relationship between a comedian and their audience). Provine (2000) also describes laughter as a highly contagious social activity. In his TED talk, Christakis (2010) also talks about the concept of *emotional contagion*.

As adults, we often find young children's jokes funny by how 'unfunny' they are, but there is still a great social connection when a child tells us a joke. We know they've worked hard on coming up with or remembering something that they want to share with us to make us laugh. Encouraging children to tell each other, and us, jokes is therefore a great way to help them form positive relationship bonds through laughter.

- **Recommended age**

  5+

- **Duration**

  15+ minutes

- **Resources**

  » Pens

  » Lined paper

- **Method**

  Ask pupils to spend a few minutes thinking about any jokes they've heard, or to make up a new joke to share, and write it down before sharing it with the class.

  Take a few minutes to listen to children's jokes as they share them with the class, and encourage children to share them with their families when they go home.

9.1.3 Acts of kindness

Acts of kindness are a wonderful way of strengthening relationships, whether with people we know, or strangers. The following activities from Chapter 2 are particularly good for strengthening relationships and connection:

» 'Kindness feedback' (2.1.2)

» 'Kindness vouchers' (2.1.3)

» 'What would you do?' (2.1.4)

» 'Support circles' (2.1.5)

9.1.4 Gratitude activities

Expressing gratitude towards other people is another powerful way to strengthen relationship bonds. The following activities from Chapter 1 are particularly useful:

» 'Daily class gratitudes' (1.1.3). You can adapt this activity by asking pupils to express gratitudes directed at other members of the class (that includes you!)

» 'Gratitude letter' (1.2.1), 'Gratitude drawing' (1.2.2), '"Thank you" card' (1.2.3)

» 'School gratitude board' (1.4.1), 'Unsung hero awards' (1.4.2), 'Gratitude email' (1.4.3)

9.1.5 Class rules

Pupils are, in many Western countries, expected to draw their motivation from external sources, such as goals set for them by others, the pressure of tests, and the fear of failure. According to Deci and Ryan's (2011) research on *self-determination theory* (SDT), external rewards, punishments and competition can reduce intrinsic motivation, whereas 'positive feedback and choice' (p.418) increase it. According to Reeve (2002), when pupils are given more autonomy, they are more likely to thrive; Deci and Ryan (2011) show that where education reform has taken SDT into account, pupils are more engaged and learn better.

Allowing pupils to set class rules is one way to give pupils more autonomy.

- **Recommended age**

  8+

- **Duration**

  1 hour+

- **Resources**

  » Flipchart and pens, or other means of noting down class ideas (e.g. whiteboard)

  » Paper

  » Pens

  » Poster paper

  » Felt-tip pens/coloured pencils/crayons

  » Scissors and glue

- **Method**

  Split the class into groups and ask them to discuss how they feel that they can best support each other, and how you can best support them, in their learning. Give each group different questions to discuss, and agree with them on how long they need to do this (we suggest 10–15 minutes). Ask them to consider questions such as:

  » *When is speaking in class OK?*

  » *What is a good way to tell our teacher we have a question or suggestion?*

  » *Is it better to work in groups or alone?*

  » *How should our desks be arranged in class?*

  » *Who is responsible for keeping the classroom tidy?*

  » *How can we help each other learn better?*

After the agreed time has elapsed, ask representatives from each group to feed their answers back to the class while you write down key points on a flipchart or whiteboard.

At the end of the feedback session, review what you have jotted down with the pupils, agree on any duplications to be removed, and you should see a set of rules emerge.

Check again whether there is agreement on these rules. You can also suggest any that you feel are appropriate, or suggest the removal of others, explaining your reasoning and gaining consensus.

Once you have agreed on a set of rules, you can work on a class poster to display them, with different groups producing parts of the poster, which can then be cut and glued onto a bigger piece of poster paper.

Encourage pupils to remind each other of the rules when there are transgressions, and make the class rules an integral part of behaviour management in class, encouraging self-regulation as much as possible.

9.1.6 Co-operative learning

Shankland and Rosset (2017) explain that co-operative learning involves pupils directly in the teaching process, promoting co-operation over competition. In cases where pupils find it difficult to co-operate, they suggest working on individual pupil wellbeing first (for activities, please refer to other chapters in this book, e.g. Chapter 1, 'Gratitude', and Chapter 6, 'Happiness and Positive Emotions'). They support this with research that indicates prosocial behaviour is enhanced by individual wellbeing.

- **Recommended age**

    8+

- **Duration**

    1 hour+

- **Resources**

  » These depend on the learning topic, so could include books, access to online resources, paper, pens, flipcharts, etc.

- **Method**

  Co-operative learning is based on dividing a class into smaller groups and providing each child in the group with a specific aspect of the teaching topic to learn about. This could be done by giving them handouts with information, access to online resources, books, and so on. The format of the information you provide will depend on the children's maturity and experience with this method of learning.

  Children then move into discussion groups with the other children who have been learning about the same topic, to discuss and solidify their understanding, before returning to their original groups and presenting their expertise. Your role is to oversee and facilitate the process.

  Additional step-by-step information on how to implement this activity can be found on the 'Jigsaw Classroom' website.[1]

9.2 STRENGTHS-BASED ACTIVITIES

9.2.1 Make a medal

This activity encourages children to look for positive traits and behaviours in other children and is aimed at improving relationships through giving and receiving recognition of positive qualities. With children aged 8 years and above, you can teach them about the VIA Character Strengths[2] first, then encourage them to use those strengths for the medals. (Allow additional time for explanation if you are using the VIA Character Strengths for this activity.)

---

1   www.jigsaw.org
2   www.viacharacter.org

- **Recommended age**

  5–11

- **Duration**

  20+ minutes

- **Resources**

  » Colouring pencils/crayons/felt-tip pens

  » Paper or card

  » Scissors

  » Ribbon or string

  » Hole punch

- **Method**

  If using the VIA Character Strengths, explain these and display them on a poster or whiteboard for all pupils to refer to.

  Explain to children that they will be making medals for each other, to recognise what everyone is good at. If you are not using the VIA Character Strengths, you could encourage pupils to recognise any strength, such as 'You are very funny', 'You are always willing to help others', 'You stand up for people being picked on', 'You are great at singing/acting/playing football', and so on. Give children a few examples and elicit more ideas from them to check understanding and get their creativity going.

  Ask children to draw medals (they can be as creative as they like with shapes), write on the name of the person they are giving the medal to and what the medal is for, colour it in and then cut it out.

  In order to avoid anyone being left out, you can either randomly allocate who writes a medal for whom, or pair/group children for reciprocal medal-making.

  Once the medals have been made and cut out, provide the children with string or ribbon, ask them to use a hole punch to create a hole and then thread the ribbon/string through. You could then have a class medal-awarding ceremony, if you wanted to really enhance the feel-good factor of the activity.

9.2.2 Secret strengths list

This is an activity created by a Positive Relationships module tutor (Rosset 2017) for the MSc in Applied Positive Psychology (MAPP) course at Anglia Ruskin University (ARU). Rosset adapted this from Bourner, Grenville-Cleave and Rospigliosi's (2014) 'Strength Notes' activity (p.112).

* **Recommended age**

    8+

* **Duration**

    15+ minutes

* **Resources**

    » Lined paper

    » Pens

    » You can also play some uplifting background music during this activity (see the 'Feel-good playlist' activity, 6.1.2), so you will need access to the song(s) and sound equipment

* **Method**

    We recommend allocating at least 15 minutes for this activity, but you can allow longer if you want pupils to have time to write on more of their classmates' lists.

    Ask each pupil to write their name at the top of a sheet of paper. They then need to fold the paper in half, lengthways, and tear from the bottom up along the fold line, stopping below their name. They will end up with two long halves of the piece of paper, joined by the untorn part at the top, where their name is. This maximises writing space for the activity.

Ask pupils to walk around for a specified amount of time, writing a few words on other pupils' sheets of paper to describe the person whose name is at the top of the sheet in a positive way. These can be general positive traits or behaviours the pupil has observed in that person, or VIA Character Strengths.[3]

Pupils start writing at the bottom of one half of the paper, carefully folding the paper once to cover their writing before moving on to another pupil's piece of paper. This way, each pupil writes their own thoughts, uncontaminated by reading what others have written. Once one half of the paper has been used up, pupils repeat the process on the other half.

In order to avoid pupils feeling left out due to not having any or many comments on their sheet, we recommend you monitor the activity closely and discreetly direct pupils towards papers that need a little more attention.

You can, of course, also write on pupils' papers, and have a paper with your name, too!

Once the activity is complete, allow pupils some time to read the uplifting documents listing their strengths. Ask them also to look out for any strengths listed more than once that particularly stand out – these are the key strengths others see in them. Do they agree, or are they surprised?

Provide somewhere for pupils to store the papers, so they can refer to them at times when they need a boost to their self-esteem, or encourage them to take them home and display them in their bedrooms as a daily reminder of the many positive qualities others see in them.

---

3   www.viacharacter.org

▓ 9.2.3 Using strengths cards

Many types of strengths cards are available to purchase, some of which are entirely based on the VIA Character Strengths,[4] while others are more generic. We use the cards created by Mindspring (2015). They use the VIA Character Strengths and we love their look and feel. They are better suited to adults and older children, though teachers have told us that, with a bit of time spent on explaining the terminology (the same terminology as the VIA Character Strengths, which may need some explanation in any case), they could be used with children in slightly younger age groups.

There are many ways to use strengths cards, and Mindspring (2015) provide a downloadable document with some suggestions. Our version is based on van Nieuwerburgh's (2017) activity set, which he used in the 'Introduction to Positive Psychology' class as part of the ARU MAPP course.

The activities described below can be carried out in one longer session, or broken up into several activities to be carried out over a number of sessions.

- **Recommended age**

  8+

- **Duration**

  15+ minutes (this is a minimum duration for each step in the sequence – allow additional time if you wish to carry out further steps in the same session)

- **Resources**

  » Strengths cards, one set per group of 3–6 pupils

  » Tables with enough space for each group to spread out their set of cards

---

4   www.viacharacter.org

- **Method**

  Start by explaining that character strengths are positive traits that are part of who we are. For example, you could ask the children to think of someone they like, and to describe them with a word that is that person's strongest positive trait. You will find they usually use character strength words to do this. Explain that the cards they will be using display 24 universal character traits that describe the positive traits of human beings across the world (Peterson and Seligman 2004).

  Break the pupils into groups of 3–6, and give each group a pack of strengths cards. Ask them to open the packs and spread out the cards, with the image facing upwards, on their table. Give them time to look at and appreciate the strengths displayed on the cards, and give them an opportunity to ask for explanations of any strengths they don't understand.

  1. Ask pupils to pick three strengths they strongly identify with – these could be the three they feel are their strongest ones – then discuss their choices with the rest of their group.

  2. Ask pupils to select the strength they are most proud of, and to tell the rest of their group about this, with an example that demonstrates their use of this strength.

  3. Ask pupils to pair up within their groups and each to pick a strength they feel represents their partner particularly well, with an example that demonstrates their partner's use of that strength. If there are uneven numbers, one group of three can work together, where pupil A picks a strength for pupil B, pupil B picks a strength for pupil C, and pupil C picks a strength for pupil A. Ask them to tell each other the strength they've picked, and the example.

  4. Give pupils an opportunity to reflect on all the stages: What did it feel like to do the activities? You can ask them to write a reflection in class or for homework, or can use this as a small group or whole class discussion.

5. Encourage pupils to commit to using their strengths more widely – for example, by finding new ways of using one of their strengths (see 'Build up your character strengths', 5.1.2), or using their strengths to help them overcome obstacles – and to help others identify their strengths.

9.3 WHOLE SCHOOL ACTIVITIES

9.3.1 Positive news spotlight

You can use school assemblies and/or school newsletters to feature individual events and achievements that pupils and staff want to share and celebrate together. Consider making this a regular feature of your whole school/whole year group gatherings and/or written school communications. You can collect the information by getting each class to provide a weekly list of highlights, or by asking individuals to let a nominated person in school know about specific news they want to share. News could be about anything good that's happened in someone's life, from a sporting achievement, to the birth of a sibling, to having received great marks in a test. This idea is rooted in research (Gable *et al.* 2004) suggesting that sharing of good news with others, known as *capitalisation*, enhances wellbeing.

9.3.2 'But-free' day

Building on the work on *active constructive responding* (ACR) by Gable *et al.* (2004) – who describe the responses we give to people's good news as either active or passive, and either constructive or destructive – Peterson (2013) encourages us to have a 'but-free' day (p.310), where we respond to everything without using the word 'but'. Shankland and Rosset (2017) stress that, although much of this research is based on romantic relationships, it is highly relevant to schools, as the encouragement of critical thinking can inadvertently lead pupils and teachers to respond in an active destructive way. Consider this example:

PUPIL A: My parents just told me I'm going to have a baby brother!

PUPIL B: Oh, that's going to make life busy in your house! Do you think your parents will have as much time for you as they have now? [or even] *But, why are you so happy about it? When my little sister was born, my parents never had time to take me anywhere or help me with homework!*

Using ACR, an alternative response could be :

PUPIL B: Oh, that's exciting. When is the baby due?

Peterson's (2013) suggestion of a 'but-free day' (p.310) could be adopted school-wide, when every member of the school community commits to responding actively and positively in conversations without using the word 'but' for the whole day.

9.3.3 Peer support

A number of schools already have systems in place for peer mentoring, such as 'reading buddies' (where older children pair up with younger children and the younger children read to them) and 'bench buddies' (there is a designated bench where children who have nobody to play with or are feeling sad/upset can sit, and 'bench buddies' go and talk to them). There are many ways in which you can encourage pupils, and staff, to support each other formally and informally within the school environment.

9.3.4 Recognising shared experiences

You could emulate the work of the 'Human Library' project[5] by setting up events where pupils, staff and parents from different cultural backgrounds or who have had unusual life experiences make themselves available for anyone who wishes to ask them questions to learn about their culture and experiences (see also the suggestions in the 'Family–pupil–teacher bond' activity, 3.3.2).

---

5   http://humanlibrary.org

You could even run an intervention to promote creating a whole school community in-group (Tajfel and Turner 2004), as suggested by Roberts (2017b). This intervention aims to re-create the Danish television advert (TV2 2017) widely circulated on social media, where separate groups of people enter a room and are asked increasingly personal questions in the form of statements about themselves. Each time a statement applies to them, they step forward, soon realising that they have far more in common than that which divides them into separate groups. Such an intervention would require significant setting up and preparation, but is worth considering in a school community suffering from deep social divisions, in order to strengthen community cohesion.

Chapter 10

GOAL-SETTING AND ACHIEVEMENT

It is important to be able to set and achieve goals, and to teach children positive, productive, and empowering ways to set and achieve goals. Research (Arthur *et al.* 2014b) by the Jubilee Centre for Character and Virtues looked at the impact that selecting life goals can have on pupils, and results showed that human flourishing, wellbeing and happiness were directly linked to goals, especially goals that are prosocial and relationship-based. This is also reflected in positive psychology, where evidence suggests that progressing towards a goal, rather than necessarily achieving it, leads to wellbeing; people who are working towards achievable dreams that hold personal meaning to them are happier than those who aren't (Hefferon and Boniwell 2011).

When we teach children how to set and achieve goals, we are teaching them *self-determination* (Deci and Ryan 2011), the skills to self-regulate, to have purpose and meaning in their actions, and a sense of self-efficacy (Bandura 1994; Komarraju and Nadler 2013; Zimmerman 2000) – the belief that they can achieve.

So, what is a goal? A goal is a challenge that a person faces; it can vary in difficulty and context. There are generally many types of goals, such as *mastery goals*, *performance goals* and *personal best goals*. Mastery goals refer to the person striving to master a particular skill or competence, whereas a performance goal is a goal that is extrinsically based, and determined by the person's competency in comparison to others. A personal-best goal focuses on improvement of the self and outperforming your previous best result (Martin and Elliot 2016). Any goal that you set is underpinned by a need, purpose or meaning, for example a desire to lose weight, to get straight As in your exams, to compete at the Olympics. Goals can be small or large and should be self-determined; we all have different needs and purpose. To successfully set and achieve goals, the most important part to focus on is not the end result (though it is important to keep that in mind), but the journey itself, and the skills that journey teaches you; skills such as *self-regulation*, *mental contrasting* (Oettingen *et al.* 2015), and *self-efficacy* (Bandura 1994; Komarraju and Nadler 2013; Zimmerman 2000).

Self-regulation helps people to manage and control their patterns, habits and behaviours (Bruhn *et al.* 2016). If we can help pupils develop their self-regulation skills – their ability to set good habits, not only in academic pursuits, but also in their relationships, health and wellbeing – we can help them thrive. As self-regulation helps with behaviour management and control, this also helps children engage with tasks and cope with the many potential obstacles that can prevent them achieving their potential (Arslan 2014).

Acknowledging the difficulties that life can throw at you is another aspect of goal-setting and achievement, and whilst we should acknowledge the potential obstacles that we could face, we should not let the negative thoughts get in the way of dreaming about what we want to achieve. This is where Oettingen *et al.*'s (2015) *mental contrasting and implementation intention* (MCII) can assist pupils in setting and achieving goals by visualising reaching their potential but remaining firmly rooted in day-to-day reality and the obstacles they may face. Future-mindedness is an important part of MCII. You visualise, in specific detail, the best possible outcome for the future. This is usually time-bound – say, in a year's or five years' time. Future-mindedness helps achieve goals as it fosters hope and optimism, as well as providing an opportunity for pupils to consider personal goals and identify the best route to achieving them (Arthur *et al.* 2014b). MCII can also assist with self-regulation in all areas of the pupil's life, and increase time-management skills – a crucial part of setting and achieving goals (Oettingen *et al.* 2015).

Self-efficacy (Bandura 1994; Komarraju and Nadler 2013; Zimmerman 2000) – an individual's own belief in their ability to complete a task – is a crucial element of teaching your pupils to set and achieve goals. Research (Komarraju and Nadler 2013) shows that, when pupils develop self-efficacy, they will place more importance on goals and will believe that they can learn new things and that intelligence is not fixed, but flexible – think 'Growth Mindset' (Dweck 2006); they will seek help when needed, and they are more likely to persist through difficulties and problems.

Goal-setting is an important skill to learn, especially as children do have the capability to set their own goals and achieve them, to the same extent as when parents and teachers identify and set goals for them (Vroland-Nordstrand *et al.* 2016).

Will it always work?

As with all work we do with children, it is always possible that a child will say, 'I don't have any goals!', or 'What is a goal?', and refuse to do an activity as a consequence. One way to overcome this type of objection would be to do the 'Class goal map' activity (10.1.2) first, so that everyone in the class understands what a goal is and the goal-setting techniques they are expected to use.

Whilst setting goals can have an impact on achievement and self-efficacy, we recommend becoming aware of the different goal-setting methods first. *SMART goals* (Doran 1981), for example, are not necessarily the best types of goals to set in education. SMART goals have become really popular since Doran coined the phrase in the early 1980s, but what many people don't realise is that Doran developed the acronym SMART for the creation and achievement of project management goals in business. Yet, people use the SMART methodology to set goals for anything from weight loss to academic achievement. It is important to recognise that what works in one setting may not work in another.

Also, remember that future-mindedness (imagining the best possible future/outcome – see also 'Best possible self' exercise, 6.1.4) is one aspect of goal-setting, but it cannot stand alone. Whilst there are benefits to thinking positively about the future, there has to be contrast with, and recognition of, the obstacles that we will face to achieve goals.

▨ 10.1 BE BOLD AND SET THAT GOAL ▨▨▨▨▨

The act of goal-setting can be exciting for your pupils; it can show them the possibilities for the future. The activities in this set are aimed at helping you explore a few different goal-setting methods with your pupils. Try one, or try them all, and work with the ones that your pupils respond to best.

▨ 10.1.1 Goal map

- **Recommended age**

  8+

- **Duration**

  30–60 minutes

- **Resources**

  » Large sheets of paper or copies of a pre-prepared map

  » Pens and pencils

  » Space to spread out

- **Method**
  Either hand out a pre-prepared 'map' or a blank piece of paper to each pupil for them to draw their own. By 'map', we mean a drawing

that illustrates a journey with a start point and end point – this is essential. You could draw one or find one online. The one we use in our RWS programme is a simple illustration of a path meandering through fields, lakes and mountains, leading up to a big sun; the start date of the goal map is at the start of the path, at the bottom of the sheet, and the goal is written in the sun at the top.

Ask the children to write down a start and end date for their goal, and write the goal itself at the end point. Along the path/road/line that connects the start and end point, ask your pupils to write down at least five steps that they have to take to achieve their goal. Encourage them to personalise their map by colouring it in.

Once they have finished working on the map, ask the pupils to turn the paper over. They are now going to think of internal and external obstacles (e.g. procrastination, fear of making a mistake, lack of supplies, or no time for the activity) they may face on their journey from the start point to the end point on the map. They need to write down any obstacles they can think of, and possible solutions to each obstacle.

Once pupils have completed this task, the maps can be displayed on the classroom walls, or at home, so pupils have a visual reminder of what they want to achieve and how they are going to get there.

10.1.2 Class goal map

• **Recommended age**

10+

• **Duration**

30–60 minutes

• **Resources**

» Large sheet(s) of paper

» Pens and pencils

- **Method**

  This is a variation of the 'Goal map' activity (10.1.1) and a collaborative goal-setting exercise, which helps to build teamwork, create bonds and improve relationships. This activity would be easier to start with a pre-prepared map, but if you have a smaller class, perhaps the children can draw their own. Once you have a map, either nominate children to be scribes and write the information down on the map, or you can take on this role.

  Discuss and decide – perhaps by way of a vote – what the class goal will be, then write this goal down at the end point. A class goal could be: 'To improve the attendance record for the class', 'To tidy the classroom every afternoon', or 'To be kinder to each other on a day-to-day basis'. Ensure that you are as specific as possible (e.g. what would an 'improved' attendance record look like and what would 'kinder' look like in terms of specific behaviours?) and that every pupil understands what is required of them. Decide on a start and end date and write these on the map.

  Now open up the discussion to decide on the steps needed to achieve this goal. You could do this in a democratic way, with pupils making suggestions, and a subsequent vote on what steps should be taken; or you could perhaps break the class into groups, with each group contributing one or two steps. Once the steps are decided, write these on the map. Repeat this process for the obstacles and plans to overcome the obstacles. Once everything is agreed upon, display this class goal on the wall and check in at regular intervals; have some regular class reflection on how you are proceeding towards your goal as a team.

10.2 SELF-REGULATION AND TIME-MANAGEMENT ▮▮▮▮▮▮▮▮

Self-regulation is an important skill to have, which includes learning how to manage your time. Teaching self-regulation and time-management will have a huge impact on your pupils' ability to achieve their goals.

10.2.1 Red light, green light

- **Recommended age**

  5+

- **Duration**

  5–10 minutes

- **Resources**

  » Large circles of cardboard in different colours, including red and green

- **Method**

  This is 'Red Light, Green Light' with a twist. You can start off playing the game as you normally would: The teacher stands at the head of the classroom, with pupils lined up at the back. The teacher alternates between holding up a large red dot for 'Stop' and a green dot for 'Go', and whoever reaches the teacher first, wins (achieves the goal).

  Once the pupils are in the habit of responding to the red and green dots, it is time to add the twist. The aim is to show them that they can break habits and manage their behaviour if they are focused and in the moment. This builds up their self-regulation 'muscle'. Now you are going to change the colours of the dots to represent stop and go – perhaps 'Stop' will be blue and 'Go' will be yellow, or purple for 'Stop' and orange for 'Go'. The children have to really concentrate and remember which colour represents which movement. Once they are confident with the concept, pupils take turns being the 'Red light, green light' controller at the front of the class.

▣ 10.2.2 Prioritise your day

- **Recommended age**

  7+

- **Duration**

  5–10 minutes

- **Resources**

  » Pens and pencils

  » Paper

- **Method**

  Hand out the sheets of paper to your pupils. Display a list of 6–12 activities on the board (use your judgement based on the age and maturity of your pupils, to decide how many), which your pupils need to prioritise. You may also choose to hand the list to each pupil as a handout. Here are some examples of activities you might list:

  » *Cleaning bedroom*

  » *Doing homework*

  » *Playing computer games*

  » *Helping parent to cook dinner*

  » *Texting your friends*

  » *Reading a book*

  » *Asking for help with a school work problem*

  » *Watching TV*

  » *Brushing teeth*

  » *Giving a hug to someone you love*

» *Doing extra reading for school*

» *Going to after-school group (e.g. Scouts, Guides, sports club).*

Explain to the pupils that they are going to re-order the activities in order of importance. Ask them to really consider which of the activities are more important than the others, and to re-order the list, with number 1 being most important to do each day. Ask them to write next to each activity why it is where it is on the list – why they have chosen, for example, that asking for help with a school problem is more important than playing a video game. This activity teaches pupils to really think about what is most important to do each day and to prioritise their daily activities based on the importance of each one.

10.3 SELF-BELIEF AND SELF-EMPOWERMENT

Self-efficacy (Bandura 1994; Komarraju and Nadler 2013; Zimmerman 2000) is a crucial aspect of being able to set and achieve goals. It means you believe in your intrinsic ability to succeed, and have the confidence to learn from mistakes and keep on trying, which links self-efficacy back to character traits and character strengths.

10.3.1 Praise the process

Teachers can help pupils realise their intrinsic abilities to achieve goals by teaching them to identify and assess what skills and strategies helped them succeed. This activity could become a daily or weekly exercise, where pupils write in their journal about a success that they had that day or week and also write about what skills and strategies they used to achieve that success. This is based on Dweck's (2007) concept of *process praise*, whereby praising a child's effort or process drives the child's motivation, whereas praising a child's intelligence leaves them vulnerable to a *fixed mindset* (Dweck 2006).

- **Recommended age**

  8+

- **Duration**

  2–5 minutes

- **Resources**

  » A notebook/exercise book to use as a journal

  » Pen or pencils

- **Method**

  Explain to children that they will write in their journal about a success they have experienced, and that they have to be really specific about the skills and strategies they used to achieve it. Encourage them, if possible, to include some VIA Character Strengths.[1] If any pupils struggle with this, provide them with an example, such as:

  > This week I won my running race. I was strong, determined and focused on what I had to do every step of the way; I persevered. I trained hard for this race, showed up to every training session, and did what my coach told me to do. I wished all of the other competitors good luck and, when I finished the race, I thanked my coach and family for supporting me.

10.3.2 Positivity post-its

- **Recommended age**

  8+

---

1   www.viacharacter.org

- **Duration**

  10 minutes

- **Resources**

  » Pens and pencils

  » Sticky notes ('Post-it® notes') or small strips of paper

- **Method**

  Hand out the pens and sticky notes or strips of paper to your pupils – they will need a few each. This activity is best done with a targeted focus, so consider what your class or a pupil may be particularly struggling with, and display a starter sentence on the classroom blackboard/whiteboard. The focus could be on academic skills, social skills, or character traits, but always start with *'I believe that I am...enough to'*. Here are some examples:

  » *I believe that I am kind enough to...*

  » *I believe that I am determined enough to...*

  » *I believe that I am zesty enough to...*

  Get your pupils to write out a few statements that show this positive belief, stating what they are able to achieve because of that skill or trait that they have. Once they have written out their positive statements, ask them either to stick these in their homework books, or a diary, or keep them somewhere where they can see them on a regular basis.

  They should keep these notes for the rest of the school year. Remind them occasionally to get them out and look at them. The aim is to reinforce their belief in their skills and traits. This will benefit them across the school year.

10.4 WHOLE SCHOOL ACTIVITIES

10.4.1 Quick step, slow step

This is a school-wide self-regulation exercise. Place cut-outs of footprints in three different colours (e.g. green, yellow and red) around the school in corridors, or even outside if you use waterproof material for the footprints. Each colour will indicate what pace the children should move at, at that point in the school. For example, green could be for walking fast (please use your judgement for this and think carefully of where it would and would not be appropriate for children to walk fast or even run), yellow for walking normally, and red for walking in slow motion.

10.4.2 School goals

It is possible to set and achieve a school goal. The goal should be decided upon by the leadership team or teachers, and should impact on all pupils and help them grow. Have a statement of the goal in the school office/reception or hall – somewhere public so everyone, including parents, can see it. Below the goal statement, keep a tracker of how the school is progressing towards achieving this goal (e.g. a picture of a target, a flower or a pathway).

Ask each year group to monitor how their year is progressing towards the goal, and at the end of each week or month, add to the tracker. For example, your goal may be for children who show perseverance in getting their homework done every night. Each teacher can easily keep track of how many pupils get their homework done on time, and contribute the numbers to the tracker. As you get through the year or term and are making progress towards your goal, the tracker picture changes (e.g. the goal gets closer to the target, the flower grows petals, or the path to the school gets shorter). Seeing this visual display of progress towards a goal will have a positive impact on wellbeing for all staff and pupils (Hefferon and Boniwell 2011).

Further Reading

Below is a list of books we think you may find useful, either from an educational perspective, or for your own personal development and wellbeing. The list includes books we have read, and books we would like to read, that we believe may help you delve deeper into some of the topics we have covered in this book. As well as a list of books, we have included a separate list of TED/TEDx talks you might find useful/interesting, as these can provide great insights in a very short space of time.

Achor, S. (2011) *The Happiness Advantage: The Seven Principles that Fuel Success and Performance at Work.* New York, NY: Crown Business; London: Virgin Books.

Achor, S. (2013) *Before Happiness: 5 Actionable Strategies to Create a Positive Path to Success.* London: Virgin Books.

Adams, M. (2013) *Teaching That Changes Lives: 12 Mindset Tools for Igniting the Love of Learning.* San Francisco, CA: Berrett-Koehler Publishers.

Annas, J. (2011) *Intelligent Virtue.* Oxford: Oxford University Press.

Arthur, J. (2003) *Education with Character: The Moral Economy of Schooling.* London: RoutledgeFalmer.

Barron, P. (2014) *Practical Ideas, Games and Activities for the Primary Classroom (Classroom Gems).* Harlow: Pearson Education. (Original work published 2008)

Baruch-Feldman, C. (2017) *The Grit Guide for Teens: A Workbook to Help You Build Perseverance, Self-Control and a Growth Mindset.* Oakland, CA: New Harbinger.

Bourner, T., Grenville-Cleave, B. and Rospigliosi, A. (2014) *101 Activities for Happiness Workshops.* Printed by Createspace, an Amazon.com company.

Brooks, D. (2015) *The Road to Character.* New York, NY: Random House.

Bruce, N. (2012) *Socially Strong, Emotionally Secure: 50 Activities to Promote Resilience in Young Children.* Lewisville, NC: Gryphon House.

Buller, J. L. (2013) *Positive Academic Leadership: How to Stop Putting Out Fires and Start Making a Difference.* San Francisco, CA: Jossey-Bass.

Csikszentmihalyi. M. (2002) *Flow: The Classic Work on How to Achieve Happiness.* London: Rider.

Esfahani Smith, E. (2017) *The Power of Meaning: Crafting a Life That Matters.* London: Rider.

Fredrickson, B. (2013) *Love 2.0: Finding Happiness and Health in Moments of Connection.* New York, NY: Hudson Street Press, Penguin Group.

Froh, J. J. and Parks, A. C. (eds) (2013) *Activities for Teaching Positive Psychology: A Guide for Instructors.* Washington, DC: American Psychological Association.

Ginsburg, K. R. and Jablow, M. M. (2014) *Building Resilience in Children and Teens: Giving Kids Roots and Wings* (3rd edn). Elk Grove Village, IL: American Academy of Pediatrics. (Original work published 2006)

Halpern, D. (2016) *Inside the Nudge Unit: How Small Changes Can Make a Big Difference.* London: WH Allen. (Original work published 2015)

Harrison, T., Morris, I. and Ryan, J. (2016) *Teaching Character in the Primary Classroom.* London: Sage.

Lieberman, M. D. (2015) *Social: Why Our Brains Are Wired to Connect.* Oxford: Oxford University Press.

Morgan, N. (2017) *Taught Not Caught: Educating for 21st Century Character.* London: John Catt Educational.

Morris, I. (2015) *Teaching Happiness and Wellbeing in Schools: Learning to Ride Elephants* (2nd edn). London: Bloomsbury Education.

Morrison, M. K. (2007) *Using Humor to Maximise Learning the Links between Positive Emotions and Education.* Lanham, MD: Rowman & Littlefield Education.

Niemiec, R. (2018) *Character Strengths Interventions: A Field Guide for Practitioners.* Boston, MA: Hogrefe Publishing.

Norrish, J. M. (2015) *Positive Education: The Geelong Grammar School Journey.* Oxford: Oxford University Press.

Peterson, C. (2013) *Pursuing the Good Life: 100 Reflections in Positive Psychology.* Oxford: Oxford University Press.

Salzberg, S. (2017) *Real Love: The Art of Mindful Connection.* London: Bluebird, Pan Macmillan.

Schoeberlein David, D. and Sheth, S. (2009) *Mindful Teaching and Teaching Mindfulness: A Guide for Anyone Who Teaches Anything.* Somerville, MA: Wisdom Publications.

Schwartz, B. and Sharpe, K. (2010) *Practical Wisdom: The Right Way.* New York, NY: Riverhead Books.

Seligman, M. E. P. (2007) *The Optimistic Child: A Proven Program to Safeguard Children against Depression and Build Lifelong Resilience.* New York, NY: Houghton Mifflin Harcourt Publishing Company. (Original work published 1995)

Seligman, M. E. P. (2013) *Flourish: A Visionary New Understanding of Happiness and Wellbeing.* New York, NY: Atria Paperback. (Original work published 2011)

Seldon, A. (2016) *Beyond Happiness: How to Find Lasting Meaning and Joy in All That You Have.* London: Yellow Kite. (Original work published 2015)

Tough, P. (2013) *How Children Succeed: Grit, Curiosity and the Hidden Power of Character.* London: Random House. (Original work published 2012)

Tough, P. (2016) *Helping Children Succeed: What Works and Why.* London: Random House.

van Nieuwerburgh, C. (2017) *An Introduction to Coaching Skills: A Practical Guide* (2nd edn). London: Sage. (Original work published 2014)

Waters, L. (2017) *The Strength Switch: How the New Science of Strength-Based Parenting Helps Your Child and Your Teen Flourish.* London: Scribe Publications.

TED/TEDx Talks

Because great content is not only found in books, we thought you may also be interested in the following TED/TEDx talks.

Christakis, N. (2010) *The hidden influence of social networks*. TED.com. Accessed on 10/10/2017 at www.ted.com/talks/nicholas_christakis_the_hidden_influence_of_social_networks.

Esfahani Smith, E. (2017) *There's more to life than being happy*. TED.com. Accessed on 27/11/2017 at www.ted.com/talks/emily_esfahani_smith_there_s_more_to_life_than_being_happy/transcript.

Loe, R. (2016) *So children can build a society, not just hold down a job*. TEDxNorwichED. Accessed on 24/11/2017 at https://youtu.be/gdzfeKTjDiA.

Schwartz, B. (2009) *Our loss of wisdom*. TED.com. Accessed on 28/11/2017 at www.ted.com/talks/barry_schwartz_on_our_loss_of_wisdom/transcript.

Temple, P. (2017) *Why should we teach Moral Reasoning?* TEDxNorwichED. Accessed on 26/11/2017 at https://youtu.be/9GHJR9OuJug.

Waldinger, R. (2015) *What makes a good life? Lessons from the longest study on happiness*. TED.com. Accessed on 09/10/2017 at www.ted.com/talks/robert_waldinger_what_makes_a_good_life_lessons_from_the_longest_study_on_happiness.

References

Arnold, B. and Guggenheim, R. (Producers) and Lasseter, J. (Director) (1995) *Toy Story* [Motion picture]. USA: Pixar Animation Studios; Walt Disney Pictures.

Arslan, S. (2014) 'An investigation of the relationships between metacognition and self-regulation with structural equation.' *International Online Journal of Educational Sciences 6*, 3, 603–611.

Arthur, J. and O'Shaugnessy, J. (2012) *Character and Attainment: Does Character Make the Grade?* Birmingham: University of Birmingham Jubilee Centre for Character and Virtues. Accessed on 26/10/2017 at www.jubileecentre.ac.uk/userfiles/jubileecentre/pdf/other-centre-papers/Arthur_2012_Character%20and%20Attainment.pdf.

Arthur, J., Harrison, T., Carr, D., Kristjànsson, K. and Davison, I. (2014a) *Knightly Virtues: Enhancing Virtue Literacy through Stories.* Birmingham: Jubilee Centre for Character and Virtues. Accessed on 21/11/2017 at www.jubileecentre.ac.uk/userfiles/jubileecentre/pdf/KVPDF/KnightlyVirtuesReport.pdf.

Arthur, J., Harrison, T., Kristjánsson, K. and Davison, I. (2014b) *My Character: Enhancing Future-Mindedness in Young People.* Jubilee Centre for Character and Virtues: A Feasibility Study. Accessed on 20/11/2017 at http://epapers.bham.ac.uk/1948/1/My_Character.pdf.

Arthur, J., Harrison, T. and Taylor, E. (2015) *Building Character through Youth Social Action.* Jubilee Centre for Character and Virtues: Research Report. Accessed on 19/11/2017 at www.jubileecentre.ac.uk/userfiles/jubileecentre/pdf/Research%20Reports/Building_Character_Through_Youth_Social_Action.pdf.

Bandura, A. (1994) 'Self-Efficacy.' In V. S. Ramachaudran (ed.) *Encyclopedia of Human Behavior 4.* New York, NY: Academic Press.

Bengtsson, J. (1995) 'What is reflection? On reflection in the teaching profession and teacher education.' *Teachers and Teaching 1*, 1, 23–32.

Biswas-Diener, R. (2006) 'From the equator to the North Pole: A study of character strengths.' *Journal of Happiness Studies 7*, 3, 293–310.

Biswas-Diener, R., Kashdan, T. B. and King, L. A. (2009) 'Two traditions of happiness research, not two distinct types of happiness.' *The Journal of Positive Psychology 4*, 3, 208–211.

Blackburn, S. (2016) 'Hedonism.' In *The Oxford Dictionary of Philosophy.* Oxford: Oxford University Press. Accessed on 31/10/2017 at www.oxfordreference.com/view/10.1093/acref/9780198735304.001.0001/acref-9780198735304-e-1453.

Bourner, T., Grenville-Cleave, B. and Rospigliosi, A. (2014) *101 Activities for Happiness Workshops*. Printed by Createspace, an Amazon.com company.

Bruhn, A. L., McDaniel, S. C., Fernando, J. and Troughton, L. (2016) 'Goal-setting interventions for students with behavioural problems: A systematic review.' *Behavioral Disorders 41*, 2, 107–121.

Christakis, N. (2010) *The hidden influence of social networks*. TED. Accessed on 10/10/2017 at www.ted.com/talks/nicholas_christakis_the_hidden_influence_of_social_networks.

Clark, S. and Marinak, B. (2012) 'The attributes of kindness: Using narrative and expository texts to confront the "casualty of empathy".' *International Journal of Learning 17*, 295–306.

Cohen, S., Doyle, W. J., Skoner, D. P., Rabin, B. S. and Gwaltney, J. M. (1997) 'Social ties and susceptibility to the common cold.' *JAMA 277*, 24, 1940–1944.

Cohn, M. A., Fredrickson, B. L., Brown, S. L., Mikels, J. A. and Conway, A. M. (2009) 'Happiness unpacked: Positive emotions increase life satisfaction by building resilience.' *Emotion 9*, 3, 361–368.

Cornelius-White, J. (2007) 'Learner-centered teacher-student relationships are effective: A meta-analysis.' *Review of Educational Research 77*, 1, 113–143.

Costello, E. J., Mustillo, S., Erkanli, A., Keeler, G. and Angold, A. (2003) 'Prevalence and development of psychiatric disorders in childhood and adolescence.' *Archives of General Psychiatry 60*, 8, 837–844.

Deci, E. L. and Ryan, R. M. (2011) 'Self-Determination Theory.' In P. A. M. Van Lange, A. W. Kruglanski and E. T. Higgins (eds) *Handbook of Theories of Social Psychology, Volume 1*. London: Sage.

Delle Fave, A., Brdar, I., Freire, T., Vella-Brodrick, D. and Wissing, M. P. (2011) 'The eudaimonic and hedonic components of happiness: Qualitative and quantitative findings.' *Social Indicators Research 100*, 2, 185–207.

Del Vecho, P. (Producer) and Buck, C. and Lee, J. (Directors) (2013) *Frozen* [Motion picture]. USA: Walt Disney Animation Studios; Walt Disney Pictures.

Demır, M. and Weitekamp, L. A. (2007) 'I am so happy 'cause today I found my friend: Friendship and personality as predictors of happiness.' *Journal of Happiness Studies 8*, 2, 181–211.

Department for Education, NatCen Social Research & the National Children's Bureau Research and Policy Team (2017) *Developing Character Skills in Schools*. Summary report. London: DfE.

Dewey, J. (1933) *How We Think*. Boston, MA: D. C. Heath.

Diener, E. and Seligman, M. E. P. (2002) 'Very happy people.' *Psychological Science 13*, 1, 81–84.

Dinkelman, T. (2003) 'Self-study in teacher education: A means and ends tool for promoting reflective teaching.' *Journal of Teacher Education 54*, 1, 6–18.

Doran, G. T. (1981) 'There's a SMART way to write management's goals and objectives.' *Management Review 70*, 11, 35–36.

Dweck, C. S. (2006) *Mindset: The New Psychology of Success*. New York, NY: Random House Incorporated.

Dweck, C. S. (2007) 'The Perils and Promises of Praise.' In M. Scherer (ed.) *EL Essentials on Formative Assessment*. Alexandria, VA: ASCD.

Edmunds, S., Biggs, H. and Goldie, I. (2013) *Let's Get Physical, The Impact of Physical Activity on Wellbeing*. London: Mental Health Foundation. Accessed on 24/10/2017 at www.mentalhealth.org.uk/sites/default/files/lets-get-physical-report.pdf.

Eisenberger, N. I., Master, S. L., Inagaki, T. K., Taylor, S. E. *et al.* (2011) 'Attachment figures activate a safety signal-related neural region and reduce pain experience.' *Proceedings of the National Academy of Sciences 108*, 28, 11721–11726.

Farbstein, I., Mansbach-Kleinfeld, I., Levinson, D., Goodman, R. *et al.* (2010) 'Prevalence and correlates of mental disorders in Israeli adolescents: Results from a national mental health survey.' *Journal of Child Psychology and Psychiatry 51,* 5, 630–639.

Fox, K. R. (1999) 'The influence of physical activity on mental wellbeing.' *Public Health Nutrition 2*, 3a, 411–418.

Fredrickson, B. L. (2001) 'The role of positive emotions in positive psychology.' *American Psychologist 56*, 3, 218–226.

Fredrickson, B. L. and Salzberg, S. (2017) 'The science and practice of loving kindness meditation.' Presentation at IPPA World Congress. Montréal, Canada.

Freudenthaler, L., Turba, J. D. and Tran, U. S. (2017) 'Emotion regulation mediates the associations of mindfulness on symptoms of depression and anxiety in the general population.' *Mindfulness 8*, 5, 1339–1344.

Froh, J. J., Miller, D. N. and Snyder, S. F. (2007) 'Gratitude in children and adolescents: Development, assessment, and school-based intervention.' *School Psychology Forum 2*, 1, 1–13.

Gable, S. L., Reis, H. T., Impett, E. A. and Asher, E. R. (2004) 'What do you do when things go right? The intrapersonal and interpersonal benefits of sharing positive events.' *Journal of Personality and Social Psychology 87*, 2, 228–245.

Grey, C. (2004) 'Reinventing business schools: The contribution of critical management education.' *Academy of Management Learning and Education 3*, 2, 178–186.

Guy's and St Thomas' NHS Foundation Trust (2016) *Abdominal Breathing.* London: Guy's and St Thomas' NHS Foundation Trust. (Original work published 2013) Accessed on 30/11/2017 at www.guysandstthomas.nhs.uk/resources/patient-information/therapies/abdominal-breathing.pdf.

Halpern, D. (2016) *Inside the Nudge Unit: How Small Changes Can Make a Big Difference.* London: WH Allen. (Original work published 2015)

Happierdotcom and Seligman, M. E. P. (2009) *Three Good Things.* Accessed on 21/09/2017 at https://youtu.be/ZOGAp9dw8Ac.

Harrison, T., Morris, I. and Ryan, J. (2016) *Teaching Character in the Primary Classroom.* London: Sage.

Hatfield, E., Cacioppo, J. T. and Rapson, R. L. (1993) 'Emotional contagion.' *Current Directions in Psychological Science 2*, 3, 96–100.

Hefferon, K. and Boniwell, I. (2011) *Positive Psychology: Theory, Research and Applications.* Maidenhead: McGraw-Hill.

Hill, N. E. and Taylor, L. C. (2004) 'Parental school involvement and children's academic achievement: Pragmatics and issues.' *Current Directions in Psychological Science 13*, 4, 161–164.

Jackson, C. and Sherriff, N. (2013) 'A qualitative approach to intergroup relations: Exploring the applicability of the social identity approach to "messy" school contexts.' *Qualitative Research in Psychology 10*, 259–273.

Jazaieri, H., Lee, I. A., McGonigal, K., Jinpa, T. *et al.* (2016) 'A wandering mind is a less caring mind: Daily experience sampling during compassion meditation training.' *The Journal of Positive Psychology 11*, 1, 37–50.

Jubilee Centre for Character and Virtues (2016) *Character Education Evaluation Handbook for Schools.* Birmingham: Jubilee Centre for Character and Virtues. Accessed on 23/11/2017 at www.jubileecentre.ac.uk/userfiles/jubileecentre/pdf/character-education/EvaluationHandbook/CharacterEducationEvaluation Handbook.pdf.

Jubilee Centre for Character and Virtues (2017) *A Framework for Character Education in Schools*. Birmingham: Jubilee Centre for Character and Virtues. Accessed on 20/10/2017 at http://jubileecentre.ac.uk/userfiles/jubileecentre/pdf/character-education/Framework%20for%20Character%20Education.pdf.

Kerner, J. and Winley, A. (Producers) and Winick, G. (Director) (2006) *Charlotte's Web* [Motion picture]. USA: Paramount Pictures; Walden Media; Kerner Entertainment Company; Nickelodeon Movies; Film Victoria; KMP Film Invest; Sandman Studios.

Kolb, D. (1984) *Experiential Learning: Experience as the Source of Learning and Development*. Englewood Cliffs, NJ: Prentice-Hall.

Komarraju, M. and Nadler, D. (2013) 'Self-efficacy and academic achievement: Why do implicit beliefs, goals, and effort regulation matter?' *Learning and Individual Differences 25*, 67–72.

Layous, K., Nelson, S. K. and Lyubomirsky, S. (2013) 'What is the optimal way to deliver a positive activity intervention? The case of writing about one's best possible selves.' *Journal of Happiness Studies 14*, 2, 635–654.

LeRoy, M. (Producer) and Flemming, V. (Director) (1939) *Wizard of Oz* [Motion picture]. USA: Metro-Goldwyn-Mayer (MGM).

Lickona, T., Schaps, E. and Lewis, C. (2002) *Eleven Principles of Effective Character Education*. Scotts Valley: Character Education Partnership. Accessed on 22/11/2017 at https://digitalcommons.unomaha.edu/cgi/viewcontent.cgi?article=1065&context=slcestgen.

Lieberman, M. D. (2015) *Social: Why Our Brains Are Wired to Connect.* Oxford: Oxford University Press. (Original work published 2013)

Linley, P. A., Maltby, J., Wood, A. M., Joseph, S. *et al.* (2007) 'Character strengths in the United Kingdom: The VIA Inventory of Strengths.' *Personality and Individual Difference 43*, 341–351.

Lounsbury, J. W., Fisher, L. A., Levy, J. J. and Welsh, D. P. (2009) 'An investigation of character strengths in relation to the academic success of college students.' *Individual Differences Research 7*, 1, 52–69.

Lumpkin, A. (2011) 'Building character through sports.' *Strategies 24*, 6, 13–15.

Lyubomirsky, S., Sheldon, K. M. and Schkade, D. (2005) 'Pursuing happiness: The architecture of sustainable change.' *Review of General Psychology 9*, 111–131.

Martin, A. J. and Elliot, A. J. (2016) 'The role of personal best (PB) and dichotomous achievement goals in students' academic motivation and engagement: A longitudinal investigation.' *Educational Psychology 36*, 7, 1285–1302.

Master, S. L., Eisenberger, N. I., Taylor, S. E., Naliboff, B. D., Shirinyan, D. and Lieberman, M. D. (2009) 'A picture's worth: Partner photographs reduce experimentally induced pain.' *Psychological Science 20*, 11, 1316–1318.

Mauss, I. B., Tamir, M., Anderson, C. L. and Savino, N. S. (2011) 'Can seeking happiness make people unhappy? Paradoxical effects of valuing happiness.' *Emotion 11*, 4, 807.

McCarthy, F. E. and Vickers, M. H. (2012) 'Positive Community Relations: Border Crossings and Repositioning the "Other".' In S. Roffey (ed.) *Positive Relationships: Evidence Based Practice across the World*. Berlin/Heidelberg: Springer Science + Business Media B. V.

McGrath, H. and Noble, T. (2010) 'Supporting positive pupil relationships: Research to practice.' *Educational and Child Psychology 27*, 1, 79–90.

Mezirow, J. (1998) 'On critical reflection.' *Adult Education Quarterly 48*, 3, 185–199.

Miller, D. T. (1999) 'The norm of self-interest.' *American Psychologist 54*, 12, 1053–1060.

Mindspring (2015) *Strengths Cards*. Mindspring. Accessed on 18/11/2017 at https://mindspring.uk.com/shop/strengths-cards.

Morgan, B., Gulliford, L. and Kristjánsson, K. (2014) 'Gratitude in the UK: A new prototype analysis and a cross-cultural comparison.' *The Journal of Positive Psychology 9*, 4, 281–294.

Nariman, N. and Chrispeels, J. (2016) 'PBL in the era of reform standards: Challenges and benefits perceived by teachers in one elementary school.' *Interdisciplinary Journal of Problem-Based Learning 10*, 1.

Niemiec, R. (2018) *Character Strengths Interventions: A Field Guide for Practitioners.* Boston, MA: Hogrefe Publishing.

Norrish, J. M., Williams, P., O'Connor, M. and Robinson, J. (2013) 'An applied framework for positive education.' *International Journal of Wellbeing 3*, 2, 147–161.

Oettingen, G., Kappes, H. B., Guttenburg, K. B. and Gollwitzer, P. M. (2015) 'Self-regulation of time management: Mental contrasting with implementation intentions.' *European Journal of Social Psychology 45*, 218–229.

Oxford Reference (2005) *Eudaimonia.* Oxford: Oxford Reference. Accessed on 31/10/2017 at www.oxfordreference.com/view/10.1093/oi/authority.201108030 95800495.

Park, N. and Peterson, C. (2006a) 'Character strengths and happiness among young children: Content analysis of parental descriptions.' *Journal of Happiness Studies 7*, 323–341.

Park, N. and Peterson, C. (2006b) 'Moral competence and character strengths among adolescents: The development and validation of the Values in Action Inventory of Strengths for Youth.' *Journal of Adolescence 29*, 6, 891–909.

Peterson, C. (2013) *Pursuing the Good Life: 100 Reflections in Positive Psychology.* Oxford: Oxford University Press.

Peterson, C. and Seligman, M. E. P. (2004) *Character Strengths and Virtues: A Handbook and Classification.* New York, NY: Oxford University Press and Washington, DC: American Psychological Association.

Provine, R. R. (2000) 'The science of laughter.' *Psychology Today 33*, 6, 58–61.

Public Health England (2017) *Children and Young People's Mental Health and Wellbeing.* Mental Health England. Accessed on 7/11/2017 at https://fingertips.phe.org.uk/ profile-group/mental-health/profile/cypmh.

Rashid, T. (2015) 'Positive psychotherapy: A strength-based approach.' *The Journal of Positive Psychology 10*, 1, 25–40.

Reddish, P., Fischer, R. and Bulbulia, J. (2013) *Let's Dance Together: Synchrony, Shared Intentionality and Cooperation.* PLoS: Blog. Accessed on 20/11/2017 at http:// journals.plos.org/plosone/article?id=10.1371/journal.pone.0071182.

Reeve, J. (2002) 'Self-Determination Theory Applied to Educational Settings.' In E. L. Deci and R. M. Ryan (eds) *Handbook of Self-Determination Research.* Rochester, NY: University of Rochester Press.

Reynolds, K. J., Lee, E., Turner, I., Bromhead, D. and Subasic, E. (2017) 'How does school climate impact academic achievement? An examination of social identity processes.' *School Psychology International 38*, 1, 78–97.

Rivera, J. (Producer) and Docter, P. (Director) (2015) *Inside Out* [Motion picture]. USA: Pixar Animation Studios; Walt Disney Pictures.

Roberts, C. (2008) 'Developing future leaders: The role of reflection in the classroom.' *Journal of Leadership Education 7*, 1, 116–129.

Roberts, F. (2017a) *A Gratitude Case Study.* Leeds: RWS | Resilience Wellbeing Success. Accessed on 21/09/2017 at RWS | Resilience Wellbeing Success: http://rws.today/ gratitude-case-study.

Roberts, F. (2017b) 'A social connection intervention for schools: Closing the empathy gap and nudging a community towards stronger cohesion and reduced prejudice.' Unpublished manuscript (available on request from fred@rws.today), submitted for assessment to Anglia Ruskin University as part of the MSc in Applied Positive Psychology course ('Positive Relationships' module).

Roffey, S. (2012) 'Developing Positive Relationships in Schools.' In S. Roffey (ed.) *Positive Relationships: Evidence Based Practice across the World.* Berlin/Heidelberg: Springer Science + Business Media B. V.

Rosset, E. (2017). Personal communication, 13 October 2017.

Sarafian, K. (Producer) and Andrews, M., Chapman, B. and Purcell, S. (Directors) (2012) *Brave* [Motion picture]. USA: Pixar Animation Studios; Walt Disney Pictures.

Schwartz, B. and Sharpe, K. E. (2006) 'Practical wisdom: Aristotle meets positive psychology.' *Journal of Happiness Studies, 7* 377–395.

Seligman, M. E. P., Ernst, R. M., Gillham, J., Reivich, K. and Linkins, M. (2009) 'Positive education: Positive psychology and classroom interventions.' *Oxford Review of Education 35,* 3, 293–311.

Seligman, M. E. P., Steen, T. A., Park, N. and Peterson, C. (2005) 'Positive psychology progress: Empirical validation of interventions.' *American Psychologist 60,* 5, 410–421.

Shankland, R. and Rosset, E. (2017) 'Review of brief school-based positive psychological interventions: A taster for teachers and educators.' *Educational Psychology Review 29,* 363–392.

Sheldon, K., Frederickson, B., Rathunde, K., Csikszentmihalyi, M. and Haidt, J. (2000) *Positive Psychology Manifesto.* Manifesto presented at the Akumal 1 meeting (1999) and revised during the Akumal 2 meeting (2000).

Sheldon, K. M. and Lyubomirsky, S. (2006) 'How to increase and sustain positive emotion: The effects of expressing gratitude and visualizing best possible selves.' *The Journal of Positive Psychology 1,* 2, 73–82.

Shlain, T. and The Moxie Institute (2017) *30000 Days – New 11 min film about Living Life with Meaning & Purpose* [Video file]. Accessed on 26/10/2017 at https://vimeo.com/226378903.

Shoshani, A. and Steinmetz, S. (2014) 'Positive psychology at school: A school-based intervention to promote adolescents' mental health and wellbeing.' *Journal of Happiness Studies 15,* 6, 1289–1311.

Smith, K. A. (1996) 'Cooperative learning: Making "groupwork" work.' *New Directions for Teaching and Learning 1996,* 71–82.

Somach, A. and Drach-Zahavy, A. (2007) 'Schools as team-based organisations: A structure-process-outcomes approach.' *Group Dynamics: Theory, Research, and Practice 11,* 4, 305–320.

Tajfel, H. and Turner, J. C. (2004) 'The Social Identity Theory of Intergroup Behavior.' In J. T. Jost and J. Sidanius (eds) *Key Readings in Social Psychology. Political Psychology: Key Readings.* New York, NY: Psychology Press.

Takano, K. and Tanno, Y. (2009) 'Self-rumination, self-reflection, and depression: Self-rumination counteracts the adaptive effect of self-reflection.' *Behaviour Research and Therapy 47,* 3, 260–264.

Tugade, M. M., Fredrickson, B. L. and Barrett, L. F. (2004) 'Psychological resilience and positive emotional granularity: Examining the benefits of positive emotions on coping and health.' *Journal of Personality 72,* 6, 1161–1190.

TV2 (2017) *All That We Share.* Accessed on 11/10/2017 at https://youtu.be/jD8tjhVO1Tc.